How to Be Educational P

Educational psychologists can play a fundamental and inspiring role in people's lives. A vibrant and expanding profession, educational psychology is becoming more influential in the lives of children and in its influence in government policy. But how do you qualify, and what is being an educational psychologist really like?

How to Become an Educational Psychologist is the first book to provide a clear, practical guide to the pathway to qualifying as an educational psychologist. Written by two educational psychologists with a wealth of experience in both education and training, and incorporating testimonials from trainees, trainers, and qualified educational psychologists, it explains every step of the journey, including advice on a suitable degree course, making the most of a training placement, how to prepare for the job interview, and the challenges of making the transition from training to qualification.

Written for anyone from current students to those interested in a change of career, *How to Become an Educational Psychologist* is the perfect companion for anyone interested in this varied, rewarding, and popular profession.

Dr Jeremy Swinson has over 30 years' experience working as an educational psychologist. He has presented his work at major conferences both in the UK and abroad, and been consulted by both the Department of Education and Science and the Cabinet Office on issues relating to classroom behaviour.

Dr Phil Stringer is currently an associate Academic and Professional Tutor at UCL, UK, where he is involved in the post-experience doctoral programme. He is also on the editorial board of *Educational and Child Psychology* and has previously been editor of *Educational Psychology in Practice*.

How to Become a Practitioner Psychologist

Series Editor: David Murphy, University of Oxford

Psychology remains one of the most popular choices for an undergraduate degree, whilst an increasing number of postgraduate courses are directed either towards further academic study in a sub-discipline, or a career in applied practice. But despite the growing numbers of people interested in a career in psychology, from A-level students to those looking for a career change, the various pathways to entry into the profession are not necessarily obvious.

The *How to Become a Practitioner Psychologist* series of books is aimed at providing a clear, accessible and reader-friendly guide to the routes available to becoming a practitioner psychologist. Providing both information and advice, including testimonials from those recently qualified, the series will include a title for each of the seven domains of psychology practice as regulated by the Health and Care Professions Council.

Each book in the series will provide an invaluable introduction to anyone considering a career in this fascinating profession.

How to Become a Counselling Psychologist
Elaine Kasket

How to Become a Sport and Exercise Psychologist
Martin Eubank and David Tod

How to Become an Educational Psychologist
Jeremy Swinson and Phil Stringer

How to Become an Educational Psychologist

Jeremy Swinson and
Phil Stringer

Routledge
Taylor & Francis Group

LONDON AND NEW YORK

First published 2019
by Routledge
2 Park Square, Milton Park, Abingdon, Oxon OX14 4RN

and by Routledge
711 Third Avenue, New York, NY 10017

Routledge is an imprint of the Taylor & Francis Group, an informa business

© 2019 Jeremy Swinson and Phil Stringer

British Library Cataloguing-in-Publication Data
A catalogue record for this book is available from the British Library

Library of Congress Cataloging-in-Publication Data
A catalog record for this book has been requested

ISBN: 978-1-138-68231-3 (hbk)
ISBN: 978-1-138-68232-0 (pbk)
ISBN: 978-1-315-54527-1 (ebk)

Typeset in Galliard
by Swales & Willis Ltd, Exeter, Devon, UK

Visit the companion website for the whole series:
www.routledgetextbooks.com/textbooks/howtopsy/

Contents

Acknowledgements

This book would not have been possible without the help and support of many of our colleagues within our profession. We would like to thank all the course leaders of a number of EP training course across the country for arranging our access to their trainees, the trainees themselves, and especially Rainart Fayette, Sophie Pitt, Leanne Greenwood, Sarah Murray and many others. Also, in no particular order, Kate Fallon, Viv Hill, Eddie McNamara, Brian Apter, Richard Melling, Stephanie James, Jonny Craig and Dan Small.

Pen pictures

Throughout the book we have included several 'Pen pictures' of a number of educational psychologists (EPs) currently working in our profession. This is to give you an idea of the wide and varied professional background and work experiences of many EPs. As you will see, we are a very varied bunch and have experience of working in many settings with a wide variety of children. While many EPs train in their twenties, it is never too late to consider a change of profession and, as you will see, a number of EPs don't begin EP work until well into middle age.

Dr Eddie McNamara

Eddie McNamara is an extremely well known EP who has work mainly in Lancashire for almost all of his career.

After leaving school he began to study Zoology at Nottingham University, 'I found Zoology a bit dry', he said, 'too much classificatory and memory work such as memorising the bones in a cod's skull'. However he had been introduced to psychology, which was a subsidiary subject. 'I found psychology much more interesting and began to get better marks in my exams and discovered that I had opportunities to have an opinion about matters. Fortunately I gained Local Authority funding to complete a Psychology degree course after completing the Zoology degree course.'

After university Eddie taught in a special school in Crosby, north of Liverpool, and after two years was accepted onto the Manchester EP training course. 'The course at that time was very exciting and we were encouraged by the course leader Jim Ward to engage in a series of classroom-based observational research studies involving teacher–pupil interactive behaviours.'

After qualifying as an EP and while working as a LEA psychologist, Eddie continued carrying out research evaluating the effectiveness of innovative behavioural interventions. Eddie was among the first practicing EPs to be awarded a PhD for his research on the behaviour management of pupils at secondary school.

He is the only practicing EP not based at a university to be awarded a Fellowship of the British Psychological Society (FBPS) based on the 1994 criterion 'has made an original and substantial contribution to psychology'.

Eddie's innovative work moved on from pupil behavioural interventions to behavioural contracting and interventions involving self-recording, self-evaluation, self-management and ultimately interventions involving the integration of cognitive with behavioural approaches.

'Fundamentally I love being an EP because I enjoy the interaction with the children and young people and the challenge of helping them achieve their potential. I feel so lucky to have had an occupation which I have, and still, enjoy so much.'

Introduction

How to become a practitioner psychologist

David Murphy – Series Editor

Welcome!

First, I would like to welcome you to this book, which is one of a series of seven titles, each of which focuses on a different type of practitioner psychologist registered as a professional in the UK. One of the things that has always appealed to me about psychology is its incredible diversity; even within my own primary field of clinical psychology there are a huge range of client groups and ways of working. The books in this series are all written by practitioner psychologists who are not only experts in, but hugely enthusiastic about, each of their areas of practice. This series presents a fascinating insight into the nature of each domain and the range of activities and approaches within it, and also the fantastic variety there is across the different areas of practice. However, we have also made sure that we have answered the practical questions you may have such as 'How long does it take to train?', 'What do I need to do to get on a training course?' and 'How secure will my income be at the end of it all?' We very much hope that this book will be interesting and answer all your questions (even ones you didn't know you had!) and further information and resources are available on our series website: www.routledge.com/cw/howtobecomeapractitionerpsychologist.

Psychology as a profession

Psychology is still a relatively young profession when compared with many long-established professions such as law, medicine, accounting, etc., however it has grown incredibly rapidly over the last few decades.

One of the first people to use the title 'Psychologist' in a professional context was Lightner Witmer who established what is widely recognised as the world's first psychology clinic in 1896 in Pennsylvania. Witmer came to study psychology after a degree in Economics and postgraduate studies in Political Science and then working for a time as a school teacher. He went on to study Experimental Psychology at the University of Pennsylvania and then at a famous laboratory in Germany. Witmer went on to pioneer the application of experimental psychology ideas to the treatment of children with specific learning and speech difficulties.

At the beginning of the twentieth century, these early psychologists saw great possibilities in applying psychological concepts to help people achieve their potential. However, even they could scarcely imagine the scale and range of applications of psychology that would exist by the beginning of the twenty-first century. Psychologists now have well-established roles in schools, mental and physical health services, prisons, police and security services, multi-national companies, sport training centres; essentially almost anywhere where there is a focus on understanding and changing human behaviour, which is, of course, pretty much everywhere!

This book is, along with the other six titles in the series, intended to provide people who are at the beginning of their careers, or those who are thinking about making a change, with an insight into the different areas of professional psychology. We hope that you will not only gain an overview of what the specific domain of psychology entails, but also a sense of what it is like to work as a practitioner on a day-to-day basis. We also aim to explain how to become qualified to practice in the area of professional psychology, right from school until being fully qualified. Furthermore, we hope to provide an idea of how careers in the different areas of psychology can develop over time and how the profession of psychology might change as it continues to develop in the future.

Studying psychology at school or college

One thing that many people love about psychology is just how broad it is. As an academic discipline it encompasses physiological workings of the brain and the nervous system, how we perceive sounds and language, how we make decisions, and the understanding and treatment of mental health problems, to name just a few areas. In recent years psychology has become the second most popular degree subject at UK universities – indeed a total of 72,000 students were studying, either full-time or part-time, for a first degree in psychology in the academic year 2014–2015.

Psychology has become not only a popular A-level choice but also increasingly an option at GCSE level. It is now possible, therefore, to take the first step on a career journey in psychology at an early age, and, if you are considering A-levels or GCSE subjects, we would certainly encourage you to look at psychology options if they are offered at your school. However, it is by no means required to have studied psychology at GCSE or A-level to follow a career in psychology. If you have already taken other subjects, or psychology isn't offered at your school, or you have decided to go for other subjects, this won't stop you going on to become a psychologist, if you decide that this is what you would like to do. Furthermore, contrary to some myths, psychology is considered a valid A-level choice for many other degrees apart from psychology; indeed it is listed as a 'preferred subject' by University College London in their general list of A-level subject choices: see www.ucl.ac.uk/ prospective-students/undergraduate/application/requirements/ preferred-a-level-subjects.

The only GCSE subjects that are specifically required by UK universities to study psychology are maths and English. A-level psychology is usually listed as a 'preferred' subject but is currently not required by any UK university for entry to a psychology course, and there is no indication that this will change. Therefore, overall, our advice would be that psychology is an interesting subject choice which can provide a good foundation for further study in psychology, or other subjects. However, psychology at A-level is by no means essential for a career as a psychologist, so we recommend basing the decision on what your strengths and interests are and also what subjects are required for any other degree options you want to keep open to you.

Studying psychology at university

The first compulsory step on the road to a psychology career is attaining 'Graduate Basis for Chartered Membership' of the British

Psychological Society, commonly known as 'GBC' (in the past this was called 'Graduate Basis for Registration' or 'GBR' for short). You will see this referred to a number of times in this book and the other titles in the series. The British Psychological Society (BPS) is the professional body and learned Society for psychology in the United Kingdom. It was established in 1901 to promote both academic and applied psychology and currently has over 50,000 members, making it one of the largest psychological societies in the world. There are two possible routes to attaining Graduate Basis for Chartered Membership of the British Psychological Society on the basis of UK qualifications.

The most common route is to complete an undergraduate degree in psychology that is accredited by the BPS; a lower second class degree classification or above is required. This doesn't need to be a single honours degree in psychology; it can be a joint degree with another subject. However, in order to be accredited it has to cover a core curriculum that is specified by the BPS, and the provision must meet certain other standards. At the time of writing there are over 950 BPS-accredited courses offered at over 125 different higher education institutions within the UK. Many of these courses are general psychology degrees; however, some focus more on specific domains such as forensic psychobiology, health psychology, abnormal psychology, sport psychology, business psychology, etc. Many are offered as psychology combined with another subject, and the array of possible options is extensive, including business, English literature, education, maths, history, philosophy, physics, zoology, and criminology, to name but a few. This range of choice could be a little bit overwhelming. However, it is important to bear in mind that virtually all psychology degrees do offer a significant choice of options within them, so two students doing the same generic psychology degree at the same institution may actually take quite a different mix of courses, albeit still with the same core psychology components. Moreover, it is also important to remember that even if the title of a degree appears very specific, the course will still cover the same core psychology content.

For a career in professional psychology, the most important issue is attaining GBC. The subtle differences in the individual course content are far less important. Our advice would be to consider all the factors that are important to you about the choice of university and the psychology course rather than getting too focused on the specific content of a course. You may wish to do a degree that allows you to specialise in the area of psychology that you are particularly interested in, and of course that's fine. However, in reality, all postgraduate professional training courses need to cater for people with a range of different psychology backgrounds so, whilst having completed specialised options at undergraduate level might provide a good foundation to build on, it is very unlikely to mean you can jump ahead of those who didn't do those options at undergraduate level.

My own experience was that I did a joint degree with psychology and zoology (I wasn't really sure what psychology was when I was choosing, so I hedged my bets!). Fairly early on I became interested in clinical psychology but I still got a great deal out of studying other subjects that weren't anything to do with clinical psychology, including many of the zoology subjects. In my final year I did an option in vertebrate paleontology (better known as the study of dinosaurs!), mainly because it sounded interesting. In fact, it turned out to be one of the most stimulating and useful courses I have ever studied, and the lecturer was one of the best teachers I have ever come across. I learned how to interpret inconclusive evidence by using careful observation and deduction rather than jumping to conclusions, and that generic skill has been very useful through my clinical psychology career. So my personal advice would be not to feel under any pressure to specialise in a particular branch of psychology too soon. I suggest you choose degree options because they are stimulating and well taught, *not* because you think they will look good on your CV. In reality, if you are applying for professional psychology training courses, what will stand out more on your CV will be really good grades, which come from being really engaged and developing a thorough understanding of the areas you are studying.

Some psychology programmes offer a 'professional placement year' within the degree. Such courses are often marketed on the basis that graduates have a higher employment rate on graduation. However, it is important to bear in mind that you will also be graduating a year later than people on a three-year course, and during the placement year most people will be receiving little or no pay and still paying fees (albeit at a reduced rate) to the university. My own personal opinion is that degrees with professional placements don't necessarily offer an advantage overall. On the one hand, if a course does offer well-established placement opportunities, this can make it easier to get that first step on the ladder; however, there are many opportunities for getting post-graduate experience relevant to professional psychology, some of which are voluntary but many of which are paid.

The other main route to GBC is designed for people who have done first degrees in subjects other than psychology, and enables them to attain GBC by doing a conversion course. At the time of writing there were 67 BPS-accredited conversion courses in the UK. Most of these lead to an MSc, although some lead to a graduate diploma; some are general in their content and are titled simply 'Psychology' or 'Applied psychology', whereas others are more focused in specific areas like child development, mental health or even fashion. However, if they are BPS accredited, all of these courses will still cover the core psychology curriculum, regardless of their title.

Since the core components are common to all BPS-accredited degree programmes, you certainly will not be committing yourself irrevocably to any one area of professional psychology through your choice of psychology undergraduate or postgraduate conversion course. In the clinical psychology programme that I run, we take people who have a range of different experiences at undergraduate level, and some who did different first degrees altogether. Of course, when you come to postgraduate qualifications, you do have to make more fundamental choices about the area of psychology you wish to focus on.

The different areas of psychology practice

The authors of each of the seven books in the series are, as you would expect, very enthusiastic about their own area of psychology practice, and the rest of this book will focus pretty much exclusively on this specific area. Our aim across the series is to provide information about what is each domain is about, what it is like to work in this area on a day-to-day basis, and what the route to becoming qualified is like. What we have not done, and indeed could not do, is say which one of the domains is 'best' for you. The answer is that there is no one 'best' type of psychologist. Instead, we hope you will be able to find the area of practice that seems to fit your own interests and strengths best. This can be difficult, and we would encourage you to keep an open mind for as long as you can; you might be surprised to find that an area you hadn't really thought much about seems to be a good fit.

Once you have identified an area of practice that seems to fit you best, we would certainly recommend that you try and meet people who work in that area and talk to them personally. Even after you have embarked on postgraduate training in a particular field, don't feel it is too late to explore other areas. Indeed, there are areas of overlap between the different domains, and psychologists with different training backgrounds might well end up working in a similar area. For instance, clinical and counselling psychologists often work together in psychological therapy services in the NHS, whereas health psychologists and occupational psychologists might work alongside each other in implementing employee health programmes.

My own journey in professional psychology started with my degree in psychology and zoology, as mentioned earlier, and led on to postgraduate training in clinical psychology and then to working in the National Health Service. However, my journey also included going on to be registered as a health psychologist and a clinical neuropsychologist, and I went on to do management training and became a senior manager in the NHS, before moving into clinical psychology training and research in leadership development. Over the years, I have worked alongside colleagues from all of the domains at various times, particularly through roles with the British Psychological Society. I have been fascinated to learn even more about other domains through editing this series and, of course, as psychology is still such a young and dynamic field, new developments and new fields continue to emerge. I would therefore encourage you to think carefully about your career direction, but regardless of whether your psychology 'career' lasts just for the duration of this book or the rest of your life, I would encourage you to maintain an open and curious mind. In the words of one of my favourite sayings, 'It is better to travel well than to arrive'. We hope this book, and others in the series, will be of help to you wherever your own unique career journey takes you!

Brian Apter

Brian has worked as an EP in both London and the West Midlands. His first degree was in Education, gained when he trained as a teacher. Brian then taught in a unit for young offenders for the next ten years.

'As you can imagine, the teaching was often very tough, but I enjoyed it. I then decided to study for a Master's degree in Special Education. There was a large element of Educational Psychology in the course, which really interested me, especially the research. While I was on the course my tutor suggested that I train to be an EP. I've never looked back. I really enjoy the diversity of the job, the challenge of working with such a wide variety of children and their families. Above all I enjoy the application of psychology. Over the last few years I have got involved with a number of research projects which have been published. I have also had the privilege of developing a strong and ongoing professional relationship with Professor Albert Bandura at Stanford University, California. This is largely conducted by email, but I have also worked with his publishers proofreading his last book. I also had the opportunity of looking after Al for a day when he visited London recently. Thinking about and applying psychology on the shoulders of such giants has become and is still a totally engrossing preoccupation.'

In the past Brian has served on the editorial board of *Educational Psychology in Practice*, the leading journal for EPs in this country, and is a member of the national committee of the DECP, the Educational and Child Psychology division of the BPS.

What does an educational psychologist do?

Today there are well over 3,000 educational psychologists working in the UK and the numbers are growing. The range of work that educational psychologists, or EPs as we like to call ourselves, do is ever widening. The number of training places for EPs has recently been increased. This is a vibrant and expanding profession which is becoming more influential, in both the lives of children and in its influence on government policy.

This was not always the case. Britain's first educational psychologist was appointed in 1913 when Cyril Burt was appointed to the post of educational psychologist for what was then the London County Council. After the Second World War, other local authorities began to create posts and by the 1960s almost all local authorities had a service. Today the majority of EPs are employed either directly or indirectly by the Children's Services department of a local authority. However, although still a minority, increasing numbers of EPs are now working privately, or in a variety of social enterprises, or for private companies, or as independent practitioners.

It is also the case that education policy is now devolved to the separate governments in Scotland, Wales and Northern Ireland and, as such, legislation, especially concerning Special Educational Needs (SEND), varies in each country. This obviously has an impact on some aspects of the work of EPs.

Whatever their employment base, since 2009, when 'educational psychologist' became a legally protected title along with the six other practitioner psychologist titles, all EPs must register with the Health and Care Professionals Council (HCPC). The HCPC issues standards of conduct, performance and ethics that EPs must follow. We will learn more about the HCPC in Chapter 4.

Educational psychologists provide a wide variety of services for children, young people, families and schools in their area. They have a responsibility for children from birth to 16 and up to the age of 25 years for young adults with complex needs. Later in this chapter we will learn more of the range of work that EPs are involved with and the large number of settings in which they work.

Whether you are an A-level student considering a career as an EP or a psychology undergraduate seeking more information about our profession, as outlined in Chapter 1, the majority of those considering a career in educational psychology have a first degree in psychology. Most universities in the UK have a psychology department but it is fair to say that the content of each course does vary from one college or university to the next and, invariably, a student will get a chance to follow a number of different options in the course, some of which might well be helpful for anyone considering becoming an EP. This needs to be borne in mind for those young people considering which university course to choose.

Although the majority of people considering becoming an EP come from those who already have a degree in psychology, that is not always the case. A number of recruits to our profession come from the teaching profession, and they are able to add to their educational qualifications in order to meet the entry requirements. That said, most potential recruits come from two groups.

One group will be undergraduate students of psychology who are considering a career as a professional psychologist and would like to apply psychology to work with children and young people. Another group are those currently working in a variety of settings with children and young people and who are considering a change of direction in their careers, and so would like to know more about working as an EP. We will deal in more detail with the qualifications and experience that any potential EP will need in order to apply for professional training in Chapter 3. Our aim for the rest of this chapter is to provide the reader with an idea of the rich and varied field of activities in which educational psychologists are involved and the environments in which they practice.

Most EPs in the UK work either directly or indirectly with local-authority-maintained schools and are part of an educational psychology service that works in that area. In recent years, as government funding for schools has changed, schools, especially Academies, have been given greater freedom to use services of their choice and therefore the pattern of service delivery can vary from area to area. This will be dealt with in greater detail later in this chapter.

Core functions

Most of the work that EPs are involved with can be looked at three different levels:

1   work with children and families;
2   work with staff in preschool settings, schools and colleges;
3   work at a strategic level with local authority procedures and policies.

For most practicing EPs, especially those at the beginning of their careers, the focus of their work will be at levels 1 and 2.

Working at an individual level includes activities such as: individual discussions with teachers about a child, individual assessment or work with a child, meeting with parents, planning an intervention to help improve the child's learning skills or attainments, and devising a programme to improve a child's behaviour. Some EPs offer a variety of therapeutic interventions for individual or groups of children, such as cognitive behavioural therapy.

An example of working at a school level would be meeting with a designated member of the school staff such as the special needs coordinator (SENCO), Head Teacher, or a member of a pastoral team to discuss the needs of the school, advise on general approaches to learning and behaviour, identify a number of children who might benefit from individual work with the EP, and to plan out future involvement. It might also include such activities as helping the school devise an anti-bullying strategy, considering new teaching and support approaches for children experiencing difficulties with literacy and numeracy, and working with a specific group of children to improve attendance or behaviour. Educational psychologists routinely provide training for teachers and teaching assistants on a wide range of topics, including aspects of child development and child mental health, and classroom management techniques. Educational psychologists may also be involved if any school or college has been involved with a very traumatic event. In recent times they have worked with schools following the Hillsborough tragedy and the Grenfell Tower fire disaster. This type of work is called 'critical incident' work. Most Educational Psychology Services have a team of specifically trained EPs who can give support to schools and to families following a major incident or a smaller-scale incident such as an unexpected death in a school.

Working at a local authority level is often the role taken by more experienced educational psychologists and those promoted to senior positions. The expertise of EPs at this level is valued in a wide range of areas, such as planning and delivering local-authority-wide behaviour plans, improving reading skills across a borough and even in areas such as the design of schools. Local authorities generally value EPs' problem-solving skills, knowledge and understanding of how systems work, and their insights drawn from psychology. Educational psychologists, therefore, are frequently invited to join working parties and policy and strategy groups.

Most EPs work within mainstream education where they are engaged right across the age range from pre-school groups and nurseries, through junior, primary and secondary schools and also, increasingly, further education colleges. They may also be asked to work in special schools and units run by the local authority, and are often employed privately by independent special schools and colleges. It is possible to specialise in some aspects of work and some local authorities have specialist posts, for example in autism, in early years work, and in profound and multiple learning disabilities. A number of EPs have dedicated time to work with 'Looked After Children' (children and young people who have been taken into care by a local authority) in children's homes and units, and to work with foster carers.

Work with children and families

To give you a flavour of the type of work that EPs do we have included three case studies. These are based on typical EP work and also outline the processes that EPs use in their work to guide their thinking.

Case 1

Louise, aged 5

Louise attended a nursery class in a primary school. She was referred by the staff at the nursery to their local EP Hemma, who was recently qualified, had been working with the nursery for the past three years, and who was especially interested in pre-school work. They were concerned that although Louise appeared very cheerful and happy in nursery, she rarely stayed at one activity for long, she could only copy a range of simple shapes with a pencil, such as a cross or a circle, and, although her speech was clear, she could not re-tell a story or tell the teacher what she had done at the weekend. When Louise was observed in the nursery by Hemma, it was apparent that although she was able to follow most instructions, she tended to look at what the other children were doing before she acted. She also tended to play alongside the other children rather than join in cooperative play and, according to her teacher, much of her play was very repetitive and involved pushing a favourite wheeled horse around the room.

Hemma decided that more information was needed about Louise's abilities in terms of her strengths and weaknesses across a wide range of her functioning, such as perceptual skills and reasoning, but especially her language skills. She therefore decided to assess these by using a standardised assessment battery of tests called the British Ability Scales (BAS). Using the BAS she worked out that although Louise's scores were broadly what one might expect of a five year old in terms of her abilities to match shapes and patterns and to copy simple abstract designs, her scores were very low in terms of her language skills, such as her ability to name objects shown to her in picture form or in her ability to follow increasing complex verbal instructions.

When Hemma met with Louise's mother it transpired that Louise had learned to talk very late. She had seen a speech and language therapist when she was two years old but, because the

(continued)

(continued)

family had moved, this had not been followed up. Her mother said that she liked playing with her toys and was especially close to her grandad.

As a result of her observations, assessments and discussions with the teacher and parents, Hemma was able to conclude that the reason that Louise was not making progress was probably because her language skills were immature. She then suggested that the way forward was to re-refer her to a speech and language therapist so that Louise's mother and nursery staff could be advised on activities to boost Louise's language development. Hemma also made a series of recommendations to staff on ways of increasing the time Louise spent on various activities in the nursery, and on helping her to improve her language comprehension and ability to follow instructions.

When Hemma visited the school the following term she learned that Louise was beginning to make progress as a result of her suggestions and those of the speech and language therapist. In the nursery, Louise was now much more involved in playing with the other children and had begun to take an interest in stories and books. It was also agreed that a more formal review would take place at the end of the school year, at which Louise's scores on various school-based assessments would be used to evaluate her progress.

The example of Louise follows a basic casework management pattern, through which EPs follow a number of stages in the way they gather information about the child and how they begin to understand the issues involved in any case.

Stage 1

First the EP has to ensure that, in most cases, there has been written agreement from the parents for the EP to become involved. For young people who are capable of making an informed decision, it would be routine practice to seek their consent to work with the EP. Next the EP has to collect background information about the child and the setting in which they are learning, in this case the nursery. This information is often contained in the school's initial request or referral for the EP to become involved. There might also be reports from other professionals who have previously met the child and her parents. The EP will clarify their own role and what expectations the staff and parents have of the outcome of the EP's involvement. In this case the teacher and parents wanted a possible explanation for Louise's slow development and advice on how to best meet her needs.

Stage 2

As a result of the information gathered, the EP will begin to form possible hypotheses to explain Louise's lack of progress. In this case, Louise's poor language skills and her lack of involvement in the various activities available in the nursery were possible explanations.

Stage 3

To test initial hypotheses, the EP then has to gather further information to validate, modify or disprove their original thinking. In this case the EP decided to assess Louise's range of abilities, and especially her language skills, to observe her interactions in the nursery class, and to gather information from her parents about her early development.

Stage 4

At this stage the EP tries to work out what they think are the reasons behind Louise's lack of progress and the factors that might be contributing to this situation so that they can come up with a plan that might ameliorate the situation. In this case the EP focussed on the extent to which Louise's lack of understanding of language limited both her participation in the various activities offered at the nursery and also her social interactions with the other pupils.

Stage 5

Here, the EP, together with the staff and parents, agree a plan of action. In this case, it involved a referral to the Speech and Language Therapy Service and interventions in the nursery to increase Louise's involvement in activities and improve her understanding of instructions. The EP made a number of suggestions to the staff, which were immediately implemented, and these comprised:

1 routinely checking Louise's understanding of any instructions;

2 working on developing language skills with Louise and a small group of children;

3 noticing when she was engaged in any activity and encouraging her to become more involved;

4 encouraging her to engage with activities when she was wandering around;

5 encouraging her to engage with cooperative learning activities with children.

Stage 6

This final and significant stage is the monitoring and evaluation of outcomes. In this case the EP was able to monitor that the referral to a speech and language therapist had been accepted and that she had been able to advise the school on a programme of activities. The EP reviewed how her suggestions for increasing Louise's involvement in the nursery were working. Lastly, a more formal review of progress had been arranged for the end of the school year.

We can see a similar process going on in this next case. However, in this case the EP involved used a slightly different approach to work with the child. This approach is called dynamic assessment. It is different from standardised psychometric tests that measure the outcome of learning. Dynamic assessment focuses on how a child learns and involves the EP taking an interactive approach and working with the child to solve problems.

Case 2

Usman is 8 years old. According to his teachers he appears quite bright. He is good at maths, joins in class discussions, and always asks interesting and pertinent questions. In the infant school he did well but he appears to have a blockage as far as reading is concerned.

He knows his letter sounds but has been very slow to learn other phonic skills such as blends (gl, br, sp, etc.) and common word endings (-ing, -out, -and, etc.). The school had asked their regular EP, Nadene, to become involved to give advice on the best approach to help with his reading as he was falling behind the rest of the class. Nadene had worked with the school for many years and they were used to her way of working.

Nadene observed him in class during a literacy session and saw he was keen to learn. She then saw him on his own. She worked with him on a number of reading tasks and also used the Cognitive Modifiability Battery, which looks at various aspects of thinking and learning. She was especially interested in looking at his memory and sequencing abilities.

While working with Usman, she provided carefully tailored instructions and feedback to help him grasp the nature of the problem and what he needed to do to produce an answer. Among other useful observations about how he approached the tasks she found that, by using this technique, he was capable of memorising and reproducing sequences. When she considered his reading skills she noticed that he could recognise simple common short words such as 'the', 'and' and 'said', but when faced with slightly more difficult longer words such as 'might' or 'shout', he invariably sounded out each individual letter sound, i.e., 'm-i-g-h-t'. He then attempted to read the word as 'mig-h-t'.

She then wrote out on a series of cards all the individual consonants, b, c, d, f, etc., and on another set of cards a series of word ends such as –ight and –out. She then taught him the word

(continued)

(continued)

ending, called a 'rime', and asked him to join up the consonants with the 'rimes' to generate both real and nonsense words, i.e., bight, dight, light, etc. He appeared to cope well with this task.

Nadene then discussed the work she had done with Usman and the strategies she had used in the dynamic assessment with the SENCO (Special Educational Needs Co-ordinator) and Usman's mother. She concluded that he was a relatively able pupil and that if his reading tasks were presented in a certain way he was able to learn. She then suggested to the SENCO that Usman used the 'onset and rime' technique, described above, in daily sessions in school and at home. She also suggested daily sessions at school and at home using a 'paired reading' approach, in which the adult and child read simultaneously.

Nadine followed up on Usman in a later visit to the school and found that he was now making better progress, was able to read a variety of 'on-set' and 'rimes', and appeared much more confident as a reader.

This case, although different in content, has followed the same six-stage model of evidence collection, forming initial hypotheses, testing these hypotheses, developing a strategy or plan to help the child, then reviewing progress.

In a number of cases when children are referred to an EP service, the main concern is with the child's behaviour. Educational psychologists have considerable expertise in helping school staff understand behaviour and to develop appropriate strategies to change behaviour for the better.

Case 3

Tom is 12 years old and in his first year at secondary school. His junior school described him as 'lively'. Reports from his last teacher indicated that although his reading, writing, spelling and maths scores were below average, he did not need any special help.

Within his first term at secondary school Tom was finding himself in trouble for disrupting lessons. School staff had used the normal range of sanctions including detentions and being 'on-report'. Although these and other initiatives had initially worked they did not appear to have any lasting effect and Tom was still the cause of considerable concern. The head of the school's pastoral team had invited Tom's parents into school and found that they were supportive of the school.

Tom was discussed at a regular meeting between the pastoral team and the EP at the school who agreed to become involved. The EP concerned, Gerry, was recently qualified but, before he became an EP, he had had ten years' experience of working in a unit for children who have difficulties in managing the behavioural expectations of a mainstream school. He asked for reports from all of Tom's teachers and noticed that Tom was well behaved in some lessons but not in others. When Gerry discussed this with Tom himself at a subsequent meeting, he explained that he preferred teachers who were very firm with him and didn't let him get away with any fooling about. He said that he fooled about to impress his mates in class and also that he 'mucked about' in French because, 'he had no idea what the teacher was going on about'.

At a lunchtime meeting, which many of Tom's teachers attended, a strategy was worked out that included:

1 Tom sitting away from his mates at the beginning of all lessons;
2 for all teachers to remind Tom of the class rules at the beginning of all lessons;
3 the French department agreed to change his teaching set so that a teacher who was especially experienced would now teach him;
4 Tom was to remain 'on-report' but, in agreement with his parents, good behaviour in class was to be linked to his pocket money at the end of each week.

Tom and his parents agreed to this new regime and a subsequent review showed that Tom's behaviour had improved to such an extent that he was taken off the 'on-report' system after only four weeks and he told the EP that he now liked French.

This case is a good example to show that, unlike the work of many other professionals such as psychotherapists and counsellors, who tend to work primarily with the client on a one-to-one basis, EPs essentially work as members of a team. An EP can only advise teachers, parents, carers and others on strategies to help improve behaviour or learning; they have to rely on and support others to carry out that advice for the benefit of the child.

Although the examples in this section have all concerned work with individual children, EPs also work with groups. Many interventions, such as planning for a successful transition between primary and secondary school, managing strong feelings, and developing friendship skills, take place with small groups as well as with whole classes, often in conjunction with a member of staff. A good example of this type of work is described below.

Case 4

When she qualified as an EP, Judith took a special interest in children on the Autistic Spectrum and they were the subject of her dissertation. In her work with a primary school two children who appeared to have social and communication issues were referred to her. One had been referred to the local Autism Assessment Team, but both the school and Judy knew this would take some time to reach any conclusion. The special needs coordinator at the school said that there were a number of other children in the school with similar but not as severe social issues. After a long discussion between the two of them and the head teacher it was decided to form a group in school to help them all. The group was called the 'Gardening Club' and it would meet on Friday afternoons. Although on the surface the group was engaged in a small garden area at the school to plant and cultivate plants, the main aim of the group was to develop social skills, cooperative learning skills and learning to work in a group, but it also gave an opportunity for the children to discuss feelings and emotions.

Judith worked with the teacher to discuss suitable activities and to share resources, and she pointed the teacher towards further training available in the authority. The group ran for two terms and was viewed by the school, and indeed by a visiting Ofsted inspector, as being very successful and innovative.

Working at a school or at institutional level

The work of EPs is not confined to individual case work. Educational psychologists provide consultation and training for staff and can be involved with research. In a school, at regular consultation meetings with the SENCO and other senior staff, a number of pupils may be discussed with the EP. In some cases an EP might agree to work directly with the pupil but in many more cases the consultation will lead to changes in how a pupil is being supported. Advice may be sought on such issues as the best approach to the teaching of spelling, the most effective way of teaching reluctant readers, or how to improve behaviour at lunchtime. Educational psychologists are frequently asked to contribute to policy development, for instance in the review of a whole-school behaviour policy, and sometimes this is linked to a training initiative so, in this example, that would be working with groups of staff to develop techniques in behaviour management. Educational psychologists offer a wide variety of training for whole staff and for specific groups. Examples of this sort of work can be found in Chapter 4, but a simple example of this type of work was when one of us was asked our opinion on a 'very difficult class'.

Case 5

Working with a difficult class

At one of his regular meetings with the staff at a secondary school, concern was expressed to the EP about one class in particular who were a cause for concern because of their disruptive behaviour.

(continued)

(continued)

The EP discussed the situation with the pastoral team, which included the assistant head teacher. As a result a meeting was arranged with all those teachers who taught the class. The teachers shared their experiences including some strategies that appeared to work for some but not all of the teachers. These were noted by the EP who then met with the class concerned and asked them what they thought could improve their work and behaviour. A lot of good strategies emerged from both teachers and the pupils, which were then implemented. The class and teachers were given regular feedback on progress. Quite quickly the behaviour of the pupils was reported by the teachers to have improved and at a discussion with the class the pupils reported to their form teacher that their teachers had also improved.

Educational psychologists have high-level research skills and these can be put to good effect in working with an institution to evaluate an intervention or teaching approach, or to shed light on a topic such as exam stress, the effects of being bought up by a lone parent, or being deferred a year, and many similar issues.

Working at a local authority or national level

Educational psychology as a profession is held in high regard at both a local and a national level. Educational psychologists are asked to contribute to local initiatives and local authority policies and plans, and to carry out research. They often work with education advisors, inspectors and school improvement managers to help improve schools that have been inspected and judged to be failing or requiring improvement. Educational psychologists may provide advice to the local authority on issues such as the best way to respond to a sudden influx of refugee children, how to raise the educational attainments of children in care, or how to improve services for the children of prisoners. Educational psychologists are usually part of a local authority's response when there has been a critical incident or traumatic event. In such cases, an EP will be required to be available at short notice to provide guidance and support.

Educational psychologists are often asked to give advice to central government on aspects of children's special needs, they have appeared before the Parliamentary Education Select Committee and have been consulted by the Cabinet Office. Through their professional association (the Association of Educational Psychologists) and the British Psychological Society's Division of Educational and Child Psychologists (DECP), EPs are represented on a range of national groups. Educational psychologists also occasionally appear on television and in the press to give their views on anything from child obesity to juvenile crime.

Who employs educational psychologists?

The majority of EPs are employed either directly or indirectly through a Children's Services Department in a local authority. Almost all local authorities have a separate Educational Psychology Service, although these vary in size and in the responsibilities they are given. They normally comprise a principal educational psychologist and, depending upon the size of the Service, a number of senior EPs and a larger number of main scale EPs (so called because they are paid on the main scale of the pay scales for EPs). Each psychologist usually works with a designated group of schools and preschool nurseries and may be asked to provide an EP service to specialist clinics, children's homes and establishments such as assessment centres.

Successive government legislation has resulted in schools increasingly being able to buy EP time from private providers as well directly from the local authority service. As a result, different employment patterns have developed.

Some local authorities have retained only a small group of EPs as direct employees and invited schools to use associate educational psychologists who, although they work in local authority schools, do so on a self-employed basis. An example of this way of working can be found in the Metropolitan Borough of Sefton, north of Liverpool, where some EPs have continued to work directly for the local authority, while others have decided that they would like to work independently and have formed themselves into small teams or partnerships and set up a 'social enterprise company' or 'community interest company'. These are essentially non-profit-making companies serving local needs.

27

An example of such a group is Catalyst Psychology in Manchester who presently employ a number of psychologists together with a number of partner psychologists who work for the group. A number of larger commercial companies have also formed to offer services to schools and parents. One example is CPA or Clinical Psychology Associates Ltd. This company was originally set up to provide psychologists to work in children's homes but over the past few years it has expanded its remit and now provides EPs to a large number of schools mainly in the Midlands and the North of England.

A number of well-known children's charities also employ EPs, such as Barnardo's and the Children's Society. Much of their work is highly specialised and often involves a great deal of direct work with highly vulnerable children and young people. A growing number of

Table 2.1 A sample week from the diary of a main grade EP

Day	Morning	Afternoon
Mon	Visit comprehensive school. Consultation meeting to discuss Years 7, 8, & 9.	Consultation and planning with Year 8 pupil, teachers and parents.
Tues	Briefing meeting of whole service. Visit FE college to see Year 13 pupil for assessment for Education Health Care Plan.	Attend autism assessment team meeting to discuss pupil. Reply to emails and telephone calls.
Wed	Visit primary school to see Year 1 child with developmental concerns and meet parents.	Training session on attachment for would-be adoptive parents. Attend meeting after school to discuss transfer of difficult boy from primary to secondary.
Thurs	Regular visit to a special school for children with complex social, emotional and behavioural needs to give advice on two pupils. Meet staff at lunchtime.	Office, write reports. Supervision session with senior EP. Attend multidisciplinary meeting about a child with autism.
Fri	Home visit about a child refusing to attend school. Work with child and parents to agree a plan for a return to school.	Office, write reports and meet with another EP to plan and prepare course for primary school teachers.

independent specialist schools in the country also employ EPs. Some of the larger specialist schools groups, such as the Priory Group or the Witherslack Group, employ their own team of psychologists, while some of the small independent schools employ psychologists on a sessional basis.

A number of EPs work as self-employed private practitioners. While they may work with a certain number of schools, much of their work comes from direct referrals from parents worried about aspects of their own child's development. Educational psychologists in private practice also receive a proportion of their work from legal firms. Such commissions invariably lead to a court report, where the EP can be asked to speak for the child. Such work is specialised and usually requires considerable experience and expertise as well as specific training.

The work of an EP, then, can be highly diverse, can involve a large number of settings, and can cover a wide range of young people from 2 to 25, of varying skills and abilities. Being an EP is not a desk-bound job. Most EPs spend most of their week away from their base, working in preschool settings, schools, colleges, assessment centres or visiting children and parents in their own homes. Each week is different. We include a sample week from the diary of a main grade EP to illustrate this diversity.

By now, you will have an understanding of the type and range of work that an EP is likely to undertake. In the next chapter we will consider both how to train to become an EP and also the qualities and experience that you will need in order to secure a place on a training course.

Sarah Murray

Sarah completed her psychology degree at Northampton University. Sarah told us,

> 'While at university I thought that I was interested in working with children. I initially worked as a Teaching Assistant (TA) and then qualified as a Teacher while working with Year 2 pupils in a local primary school. I really enjoyed it. The idea of being an Educational Psychologist had always been in the back of my mind, when I saw an advert for the post of Assistant Educational Psychologist working in Leicester. I applied. I was fortunate enough to get the appointment and then spent 15 months on a special project which involved supporting children and families from disadvantaged families through group therapeutic approaches. I was part of the team that evaluated the project. Working as an assistant EP gave me the opportunity to work closely with EPs and develop my understanding of the research element of an EP's work.'

Sarah is a former student on the Birmingham course.

How to train to be an educational psychologist

In this chapter we will learn about the training of EPs: the various training programmes in the UK, the types of experience you can expect on the programme, and the qualifications and work experience you will need to have in order to apply. We can assume that, having read Chapters 1 and 2, you are beginning to have some idea of what is involved in being an EP. Before you begin to apply for any programme you will obviously need to ensure that you have the necessary qualifications and experience. Since you will be making a considerable commitment to becoming an EP, you will also need to be certain that it will be the career for you. How can you be certain? These are some important steps that you can take.

Step 1: meet an educational psychologist

We would strongly advise you to talk to a real live EP to learn more about the Educational Psychology Service in your area and what the EPs do. If you are working in education as a teacher, teaching assistant, pastoral support officer or learning mentor and you are based in a school, the first obvious port of call will be the EP who visits your school. Educational psychologists are approachable people (it is part of the job), therefore find out who in your school liaises with the EP. Ask them if you can be introduced to the EP when they are next in school with a view to arranging to meet them to discuss your interest. If you don't work in a school then we suggest you email the principal educational psychologist or telephone your local service and ask to meet an EP. You will find the details on the local authority's website.

At that meeting we would suggest that you ask about the possibility of work shadowing, however briefly, so that you can get a feel for the work. This may be difficult for teachers working in schools but EPs often work at some point during the school holidays so some sort of arrangement is often possible.

Step 2: learn as much as possible about the work of an EP

We can assume that by the end of reading this book you will know a great deal about the work of EPs. However, we also suggest that you read other published books and journals written and read by EPs to get an up-to-date picture of our discipline. The most read journals by EPs are *Educational Psychology in Practice* and *Educational and Child Psychology*. These journals are available in most university libraries and will give a flavour of the type of research and developments in our field. If you cannot easily get library access then the same EP that you speak to in Step 1 (see above) will more than likely be willing to lend you journals or books.

We would also direct you to two websites, those of The Association of Educational Psychologists (AEP) and the British Psychological Society (BPS) who both have extensive pages on the work of EPs and training.

Step 3: contact the local training programme

If you are convinced that training as an EP is for you, contact the training programme nearest to you. Ask if there are any open days or evenings or ask if you can meet with the programme director or a member of the tutor team. We talk a bit more about this below.

Step 4: applying for a course in England

You need to be aware that applying to train as an EP does vary across different parts of the United Kingdom (UK) and different rules apply in England, Scotland, Wales and Northern Ireland.

We will describe the procedure for England first and then look at how it varies in other parts of the UK. Since the training arrangements can change, it will be important that you get the most up-to-date information that you can.

In England the application system is coordinated by the Association of Educational Psychologists (AEP), who are the professional association to which the vast majority of EPs belong. Therefore, your first step is to visit their website and to download the information.

The first information to catch your eye will be the entry qualifications needed to apply for a course. These are twofold:

1   A first degree in psychology or the equivalent.
    You will have learnt in Chapter 1 about degrees in psychology. This means that the main area of study of your degree has been in psychology and that the British Psychological Society (BPS) has accredited it. If this is the case you will be eligible for graduate membership of the BPS. If you have any doubts about your qualifications it is important that you clarify the situation with the BPS. They will be able to tell you if your degree qualifies. Competition for places on the training course is stiff and therefore most courses prefer candidates to have at least a 2.1 degree.

If your first degree either does not include enough psychology to qualify for accreditation by the BPS or was in a subject other than psychology, then you may consider taking a BPS-accredited psychology conversion course. You will find details of conversion courses on the BPS website. Another option is to register with the Open University and either take a degree course or complete a number of course units in psychology, which, together with your first degree, may be enough to qualify you for graduate membership of the BPS.

Another route for qualification that has been used by a number of non-psychology graduates is to study part-time for a Master's degree in an aspect of psychology. This route has been taken by a number of EPs who have an education degree.

Finally, you may have a degree from a university abroad. In 2014 the BPS started to accredit UK degrees that are delivered internationally. If you completed an accredited course and meet the eligibility criteria then you will automatically be awarded Graduate Basis for Chartered

Membership (GBC). If you are neither a UK applicant nor have completed an accredited course, then the BPS will assess you individually to decide if you are eligible for graduate membership.

If you have any doubts about your qualifications it is essential that you contact the BPS as early as possible to ensure that your qualifications meet their criteria.

2   At least one year's experience of working with children or young people in a structured setting.

In the past EPs had to train and work for a minimum of two years as a teacher in order to qualify for EP training. Since 2006 all training in England, Wales and Northern Ireland has become a three-year doctoral programme and the requirement to train and work as a teacher was dropped. However, there are a number of options you could consider to fulfil this requirement.

In our view, experience working in a school as a teacher is the most valuable experience for a potential EP. Trained teachers have wide knowledge of education theory and practice and experience of planning and delivering lessons, working with parents and with individual children, some of whom may have educational difficulties of some sort. It is worth pointing out that, according to tutors who run the courses, it is still the case that around half of those applying to become an EP are qualified teachers who have had experience of working in schools.

The other main group of applicants is people who have experience of working in schools as teaching assistants. Teaching assistants are often appointed to work with a specific child or a number of children who have special educational needs, which is the group of children in which EPs also have a particular interest. Therefore, teaching assistants can have valuable experience of working in schools and liaising with teachers and others to plan out individual programmes.

Other types of experience that may be valuable includes work in schools as a learning mentor, behavioural support worker or pastoral support officer. All of these jobs are usually found in secondary schools helping young people with their learning or behaviour. Some people apply for training with experience as youth workers or of working as care assistants in a children's home or residential school with young people who may have special needs or are being 'Looked After' by the local authority.

Other options could include training and experience as a speech and language therapist, a school counsellor or a social worker. Probably the best type of experience would be to find a post as assistant educational psychologist. These posts are rare, but in the past have been offered by a small number of Education Authorities including Essex, Hampshire, Buckinghamshire and Kent. They involve working as an assistant to a qualified EP. Assistant EPs cannot cover the full range of responsibilities of an EP and have to work under the close supervision of a qualified EP. Nevertheless, the type of experience you would gain in such a post can be invaluable, but it is worth reiterating that such posts are very rare and are invariably only available to applicants who have already had experience of working with young people.

The key element of all of these experiences is that you have worked directly with children or young people. This may of course include some types of experience that have been acquired through work as a volunteer. Indeed such voluntary work not only shows a commitment to work with children but may give you valuable experience of working with those with a specific difficulty, such as working with autistic young people.

If you have any doubts about whether your work experience is valid, then you should first consider the training requirements listed on the AEP website and then, second, contact one of the university programmes.

Step 5: choosing a course

When you apply, you will be asked to select three programmes. The courses in England are distributed across the country so they are accessible to most potential students. A list of programmes is available from the AEP website. At the time of writing they are:

Birmingham University

Bristol University

Exeter University

Manchester University

Newcastle University

Nottingham University

University of East Anglia

Sheffield University

Southampton University

London: University College London

The Institute of Education

The Tavistock Institute

The University of East London

Each programme follows a broadly similar curriculum, which will be outlined later, but obviously there can be big differences in terms of styles of delivery.

In the first instance we would recommend that any potential trainee EP look at the details of these programmes that are available on each university's website. In addition, and as we suggested earlier, a programme may hold an open day or evening where you would have a chance to learn more about the course and, more importantly, have a chance to meet the course tutors and some of the current trainee EPs.

Application process

In England there is a centralised application process, which is at present run by the Association of Educational Psychologists (AEP). You must first register an interest via their website (www.aep.org.uk/Training). You will then be directed to the Educational Psychology Funded Training (EPTF) website and their online application system. You will be required to pay a small administration fee (£25 at present).

At present the recruitment timetable is as follows.

The exact dates will vary year to year but are explained in a detailed handbook which an applicant can download from the AEP website.

Table 3.1 The recruitment timetable

Online application system live and applications can begin. You have to provide contact details for your referees and submit your preferred choice(s).	Early October
Referees have to submit reference by deadline.	Late November
Application deadline.	Early December
Courses draw up shortlist and interview candidates.	January–March
Courses offer places to chosen candidates.	Early April
Deadline for accepting place.	Mid April
Reserve list deadline.	Late April
After interview a small number of applicants may be offered a place on the reserve list, in which case the outcome of their application will not be finalised until late April.	

The timetable for the process begins almost a year before you can expect to start the course. As with almost all online application systems, this is a very strict timetable that is immutable. You also have to provide two references, one academic and one related to your work experience, so it is best to have these organised well in advance. Therefore, any applicant would be wise to make themselves fully aware of all the deadlines and ensure that they and their referees are able to submit the necessary information on time. On one occasion one of the authors was asked to submit a reference at only three days before the deadline.

All programmes are over-subscribed and therefore competition is very stiff. If you are applying for a course you would be advised to take considerable care over all aspects of your application:

* It is important that you include all aspects of your previous experience that have relevance to working with children and, in particular, how you have applied psychology in this work.

* It is important that you ensure that your referees know about the particular programmes that you are applying for and that they emphasise those of your qualities that they think would be valuable in this profession.

* If you are given an interview, it is important that you prepare well in terms of your knowledge of the profession but also that you project those qualities that suit you to the profession.

Ideally we would suggest that you ask a friendly EP to conduct a mock interview. We accept that this might not be easy to arrange although, if you are working as an assistant EP, it will be more straightforward. Your preparation should include thinking yourself into the work of an EP and into being a member of a training programme. As one programme director told us:

> We are not looking for know-it-alls. We are looking for people who are good listeners, people that show empathy, with children and adults. We expect them to have a good psychological knowledge but above all some insight into how that knowledge can be applied to situations they have already experienced in their work with children. Educational psychologists need very good interpersonal skills and we try and pick this up during the interview, but also in a number of group exercises and problem-solving activities that we put any potential trainee through on interview day.

Should you be successful you will be offered a place in early April and can begin to anticipate the year to come.

Who's who on the training programme

Every programme is delivered in the university by a tutor team who are all qualified and experienced EPs. This is led by a programme director whose major work commitment is to the course. The rest of the team comprises associate tutors, usually working for a local authority and seconded for part of the week to the team, and field tutors, based in a local authority and supervising trainee EPs in the first year when they are on placement. In addition to input from the tutor team, trainees will receive seminars and workshops from speakers with particular areas of expertise outside the tutor team, in particular lecturers based in the university and educational psychologists, often from a nearby local authority.

Structure of training

Training to be an EP is a five-year commitment. The first three years involve the university-based doctoral degree followed by a minimum of two-years employment in England. As we have already said, each programme varies to some extent but a typical pattern would be:

Year 1

This is university-based, where trainees build up their skills and knowledge in a series of workshops and seminars. Much of the training is practically based and follows a guided practice-based learning model in which students and tutors work together on scenarios typically encountered in practice. This first year will also contain a number of carefully supervised placements in an educational psychology service, and sometimes in other settings, where the trainee can begin to learn about the context of EP work and begin to understand the link between theory and practice. These placements are usually in services near the university and are supervised by fieldwork tutors.

Towards the end of Year 1 you will be allocated a training place, usually with a local authority service.

Years 2 and 3

During this period you will be working as a Trainee Educational Psychologist. As such you will spend three days a week working in the field, gradually taking on more responsibility, but always under the supervision of a nominated EP within the service. These placements are very carefully planned to provide you with the wide range experience that you would expect to have when you are fully qualified. The majority of the work will therefore be in mainstream schools. Over the course of the two years you will be expected to take more responsibility for the planning of your own work. You will also have an opportunity to take an interest in a specialist area, such as work with a behavioural unit or perhaps an assessment centre. Such specialist work can be invaluable as it can give you an opportunity to work in a specialist setting, which you can then study in greater detail and that could be included as part of your dissertation. As a trainee you will be expected to meet with your supervisor on a regular basis and, of course, with your university tutor. The remaining two days a week are university-based and continue with seminars and workshops as well as with working on your thesis.

At the end of the three years, when you have met and passed all the course requirements, you will need to register with the Health and Care Professionals Council, the regulatory organisation for EPs, and you will then be able to use the title of Educational Psychologist.

What will I study on the programme?

It goes without saying that each programme is unique in terms of the emphasis that it places on aspects of knowledge and practice. It is important that any potential EP examines each course carefully in terms of its philosophy, approach and potential practice. However, every programme does follow a broadly similar curriculum, which has been agreed by both the British Psychological Society (BPS) and the Health and Care Professionals Council (HCPC).

It is true to say that most of the theoretical and knowledge-based content of the course occurs in the first year of training. Typically the content in the first year includes the following.

Approaches to assessment

You will receive a thorough grounding in a broad problem-solving approach to sensitive and culturally competent assessment and then become familiar with a range of particular approaches to gathering assessment information, ranging from interview techniques to tests.

Aspects of child and adolescent development

This includes learning about cognition, memory and intelligence, language development, including the effects of bilingual language development, dyslexia, Attention Deficit Hyperactivity Disorder, neuro-psychological disorders and autistic spectrum conditions. You will be expected to study each of these areas in some detail. For example, when learning about autism, you will study the history of the condition, the characteristics that are used to diagnose the condition, the impact that the condition has upon learning, the types of educational provision that are available for children with the condition, and the attempts that have been made to evaluate the success of various education programmes made available for such children.

Learning

This includes detailed study of the development of children's literacy and numeracy skills and especially an analysis of the types of programmes that have been developed to help children with literacy and numeracy difficulties.

Social and emotional development

This includes the importance of children's emotional well-being and the development of social behaviour and the impact this has on their learning. Relationships with teachers, parents and peers are studied in detail, as well as the wide range of social, emotional and behavioural difficulties experienced in childhood and adolescence

Aspects of educational practice

This section includes the study of achievement in schools, attempts to reduce social exclusion, promoting inclusion of children with Special Educational Needs and Disabilities (SEND), and the success or otherwise of attempts by EPs and others to improve the performance of schools.

The profession of educational psychology

This includes the study of working with schools and multi-agency teams, ethical issues in practice, an exploration of effective school-based and individual interventions, and issues such as managing professional development.

Content in Years 2 and 3

In Years 2 and 3 there is less academic and knowledge-based content. However, trainees would be expected to cover a wider range of topics including: children with profound and multiple learning difficulties, physical and sensory difficulties, challenging behaviour, effective family interventions, effective preventative and early interventions, and tackling disadvantage. Also in these years there is a chance to study a wide range of methods of inquiry, that is, the wide range of ways that psychologists attempt to examine the effectiveness of interventions and examine the causes and amelioration of educational issues. This invariably involves an examination and comparison of what is called qualitative and quantitative methods of enquiry.

Trainees are encouraged to explore some cases in great depth, which may take the form of a detailed 'case study' that can form part of their examination. Most courses will also consider aspects of the role of EPs at special educational needs and disabilities tribunals and in court work, give an opportunity for trainees to carry out an in-depth literature review, and to take part in some aspect of teacher professional development.

How will I be assessed on the course?

The assessment of trainee EPs varies between courses but generally a student can expect a number of assignments over the three years. These would typically include:

- In Year 1, three research-based assignments of around 10,000 words on topics such as, for example, evaluating the social, organisational and ecological context of children's learning, and a systematic literature review, usually related to the needs of the service.

- In Year 2 further assignments will be set. A number of courses expect an evaluation of an intervention as part of the year's assignments, others require a detailed and thorough literature research. A recent example from Manchester was an assignment that asked the trainee to write a paper on 'The prevalence of autism in the population' – a paper that was then used by his local authority to help plan provision.

• At the end of Year 3 you will be expected to produce a thesis based on original research. Therefore, much of Years 2 and 3 will involve examining the literature around your chosen area, designing and refining your method of research, and, of course, carrying out the research itself and finally writing it up into a bound thesis. The length of the thesis does vary from one course to another. Some courses only expect 20,000 words while on others it can be up to 40,000 words. The topics that have been studied vary a great deal. Examples of recent theses are included below.

Recent EP theses

- Maternal attribution in the treatment acceptability of interventions for problem behaviour in children with ADHD.
- Exploring children's writing during therapeutic storytelling interventions.
- Examining relationships between sources of self-esteem and aggression in adolescents.
- Understanding the role of metacognition and working memory in maths achievement.
- Examining the relationship between specific praise and pupil engagement in numeracy hour.
- Exploring the emotional labour experienced by teachers of looked-after children.
- Gay fathers and the interface with primary education: an interpretative phenomenological analysis.
- An exploration into how collaborative problem-solving groups can change teachers' practice.
- Teachers' achievement goals as predictors of classroom instruction and differences in teaching high- and low-attaining classes.
- Storytelling into writing: effects on pupils' composition skills and self-efficacy.
- What factors influence teachers' acceptance of evidence-based interventions?

(continued)

(continued)

- Never too young for power: effects of social power on cognitive processing and social competence in pre-schoolers.
- What are friends for? The perceptions of young people in care about peer relationships.

In addition, each trainee is expected to produce a 'Professional Practice Portfolio'. This will include all the work they have carried out in their various placements over the course of the three years. Much of this will inevitably include reports of individual cases they have been involved with, but also the training they have carried out in schools, consultations they have had with teachers, schools and families, or interventions with schools, establishments or even services.

Lastly there will be a series of reports from the three placement supervisors on the work of the trainee, as well as observations by their tutor on their work on placement.

The fall-out rate of trainees is very small indeed. The overwhelming majority of trainees that start the course successfully qualify as EPs.

Costs

At present the cost of the training course is covered by the Department for Education (DfE) and courses are administered through the National College for Teaching and Leadership (NCTL). They will pay the universities the course fees for all of the three years. In addition, in the first year (Year 1), a bursary is payable to each student. At present (2018), this bursary is around £16,000. However, it is tax free and therefore, in real terms, is worth more. One important caveat to bear in mind is that one condition of the bursary is that, once qualified, EPs in England are expected to work for at least two years in this country.

In Years 2 and 3, when you spend more time on your practice placement, responsibility for paying you falls onto the placement provider. This is either in the form of a bursary or in terms of a salary paid at the rate for Trainee EPs. Details of this pay rate can be found on the AEP website.

It is possible for a student to self-fund a place on a training course. If you were to consider this option it is important that you contact the relevant university directly to find out if such places are available. Very few students take this option as it is very expensive. Some universities are involved with the training of EPs from around the world but, again, this would have to be negotiated with each university.

Wales and Northern Ireland

Responsibility for education in Wales and Northern Ireland has been devolved to their respective Assemblies. Therefore they have a separate legislation covering all aspects of education policy and practice. In fact, in both cases, the model of education is very similar to that in England, although there are important variations covering the provision of children with special educational needs and disabilities.

The course in Wales is at Cardiff University and in Northern Ireland it is based at Queens University Belfast. In both cases the pattern of training is based on the English model. The course at Queens places a strong emphasis on intervention skills including: counselling, Video Interactive Guidance (VIG), Cognitive Behavioural Therapy and Motivational Interviewing. The course in Cardiff is known for developing a systematic template for casework known as a 'Constructionist Model of Informed Reasoned Action' (COMOIRA).

Both these courses lead to a professional qualification at doctoral level, Doctor in Educational Psychology (DEdPsych), and recognition by the Health and Care Professions Council. Therefore any EP trained on these courses is qualified to work anywhere in the UK.

Applications for these two courses can be made directly to each university and follow a similar timetable to that of the English courses. The entry requirements are also very similar, i.e., a good degree in psychology, usually at least a 2:1, and appropriate and sufficient experience of working with children and young people in an educational, social services or community setting, for usually in excess of one year's duration. Both courses are funded directly by their respective governments, who pay the university fees and a bursary to each trainee over the three-year period at a similar rate to that paid to English trainees. Potential recruits for these two courses are invariably people already working in the respective region and after qualification, like trainees in England, they are expected to work locally for at least two years.

If you are considering applying to either of these courses you are advised to consult the course's website for up-to-date information and an application form.

Scotland

Training in Scotland is markedly different from the training elsewhere in the UK and is in two stages. The first two years are university-based and the third year involves working for one year as a probationer EP supervised by a qualified EP.

Stage 1

The Scottish training programmes are based at Dundee University and the University of Strathclyde in Glasgow. These courses are both two-year fulltime programmes leading to a Master of Science (MSc) degree. They are very similar and are run on alternative years. At present Dundee courses start in the September of even-numbered years and Strathclyde courses on odd-numbered years. You will need to check this out before you start to apply.

The entry requirements are a good degree in psychology, 2:1 or above, and at least two years' experience of working with children in a structured setting. As in England, many of the applicants have teaching experience but other types of experience are considered. If you have any doubts about the suitability of your experience please contact one of the universities.

In the first year the programmes start with a period of induction, followed by a block placement in a local authority service. For the rest of the first and second years two days a week are spent on placement with a local EP service, while the rest of the week is spent at the university. As with the other UK programmes, much of the study involves 'problem-based learning' in which trainees work with their tutors through the type of difficulties and problems EPs are likely to encounter in their practice. An attempt is then made to integrate this practical experience with theory and to look at the wider socio-economic context in which children learn. The content of the courses is similar to those in England, Wales and Northern Ireland and the trainees complete various assignments and produce a 'professional practice portfolio' containing written accounts of the work they have completed on their various placements. They also have to provide a thesis, but as these are only at Master's level they are not as long or in as much depth as the theses from the courses offering doctoral-level programmes, but, nevertheless, the thesis is usually in excess of 20,000 words.

Both universities run open days when any potential trainee can meet staff and trainees and find out more about the courses. Both courses also have extensive information on their respective websites.

Fees

In the past the Scottish Government has funded both courses. However, at present, this is no longer the case and trainees have to find their own course fees, which at present are around £9,000 a year. Although some scholarships are available, most students have to find the money themselves as well as pay their own living expenses. Professional development loans are available for Scottish students. We also understand that recently a small number of trainees have been seconded during their training by their local authorities. Therefore it may be worthwhile for any potential Scottish trainee to contact their own authority, especially if they know there is a shortage of EPs in the region.

The lack of funding for the training of EPs in Scotland can make the decision to train to be an EP a difficult one. Since the Scottish Government withdrew financial support the number of applicants to the courses has fallen, which has had a knock-on effect on the number of EPs on the course. This is despite the findings of an enquiry into Educational Psychology in Scotland, *The Currie Report* (2002), which argued for more training places and increased funding.

Stage 2

In order to become a registered educational psychologist it is necessary to complete the British Psychological Society Qualification in Educational

Psychology (Scotland)(Stage 2). The qualification is conferred by the British Psychological Society (BPS) on successful completion of one full-time (or equivalent) year of supervised practice in the employment of a local authority psychological service and the submission of a portfolio of competence.

During this year trainees are known as educational psychologist (probationer), and usually apply for paid posts in a local authority psychological service where they work under the supervision of an experienced EP. Their supervision has to be on a regular basis, records are kept of their activities and a log is made of the cases and other work that they have been involved with. The portfolio of competence submitted to the British Psychological Society for approval consists of a file of their work, together with a log of their activities and a report from their supervisor.

Once the BPS Qualification is completed, the newly qualified EP will be eligible to register with the Health and Care Professions Council (HCPC) and is free to apply for any educational psychologist post in the UK. The vast majority of Scottish-trained EPs continue to work in Scotland, but a number have migrated south and, equally, a number of English EPs now work in Scotland.

Final words

The training to be an EP is long and at times arduous but few trainees drop out. The retention rate for almost all courses is 100%. In the following chapter we relate the experiences of trainees to give you a feel of what to expect.

Leanne Greenwood

Leanne completed her psychology degree at Manchester Metropolitan University. It was while she was there that she learned about becoming an EP when she attended an open day at Manchester University.

She therefore got herself a job as a Learning Assistant at a comprehensive school in the city. She worked with a wide variety of children with both learning and behavioural issues. She told us that she applied for a place on the course in four successive years. 'The tutors on the course were very supportive and told me the type of experience I needed to be successful', she said, 'and the head at my school was also encouraging and allowed me to have experience of working with a very diverse group of children'.

Leanne went on to complete the Manchester course.

The training experience

In the previous chapter you learned about the structure and content of the training courses. In this chapter we will cover the training experience, preparing for an interview, the ethics and values of educational psychologists, what you might expect during the three years of training, and financing training. A significant focus will be on how trainee EPs themselves describe their experience of the three years of their training and so we invited a number of trainees from several courses to tell us what their training was like from a personal perspective.

Experience prior to applying to training programmes

The trainees we interviewed had a variety of previous career experiences before they applied for their course. The vast majority had experience of working in schools, as either teaching assistants, learning mentors or qualified teachers. A number of the teaching assistants had been general classroom assistants but a large number had experience of being assigned to individual children with a specific special educational need. One trainee told us,

> *I was appointed to support a small boy with Autism. Up until then I had no experience of young people with that condition, but working with him got me really interested in the condition and really persuaded me to learn more and led me to decide to train as an EP.*

Another trainee was appointed as a teaching assistant in the learning support department of a large high school. She told us,

My main job was to help students with literacy problems. As a result I gained a lot of experience of reading problems including dyslexia. This experience was important in getting me a place on the course and has subsequently helped me in my work with working with secondary schools.

Yet another said,

After my undergraduate degree in psychology, I worked as a teaching assistant for three years in a few different primary schools to try and get a range of different experiences. The majority of this time was spent as a TA for a set of twins who needed extra support with the development of their speech and language skills. All of this experience was with primary-aged pupils. Therefore, I knew when I started the course that there was a real gap in my knowledge when it came to working with secondary-aged pupils.

The former teachers we interviewed had been in the classroom for between two and 12 years. The majority had experience of working in primary schools. One trainee from the Birmingham course said that she had been a teacher of Year 3 children before training. She said that she had always been interested in educational psychology as a career so she was pleased when she saw an available post as an assistant educational psychologist with the Northampton Psychology Service.

The trainee job was a great experience. It involved evaluating a project with family support workers who had used a technique called 'Video Interactive Guidance' to help enhance parenting skills in families by allowing them to reflect on their child-rearing practice. It was actually called 'Video Enhanced Reflective Practice' or 'VERP' for short. I have no doubt that my experience as an assistant EP got me onto the course. It not only gave me an opportunity to work with a very interesting project and gave me experience of evaluation, but also an opportunity to work alongside a team of educational psychologists, who were all so helpful and supportive.

She went on to say that she thought that, as a result of her experience, she had an advantage over other trainees at the start of her training.

The trainees that we spoke to made a decision about which course to apply to either based on the course closest to where they were living or they were willing to relocate. For those willing to relocate or for those living in and around London there is clearly a greater choice. The website for each training course will provide detailed information about the structure and content of the programme. We will not attempt to summarise the similarities and differences here. Historically, all courses develop slightly different emphases, not least through the interests of the programme director and course team, although it is useful to bear in mind that all courses have to be accredited by the British Psychological Society according to set criteria, and so the end results will be broadly similar in terms of the skills and experiences that are developed.

All the trainees we spoke to said that they had been able to attend the open days where a course had put one on. They thought that this was essential in that it gave an opportunity not only to learn about the course and meet the tutors, but, above all, to get a feel for the course and an idea of what the tutors expected from the trainees over the three years.

A number of trainees told us they had applied for two or three successive years before securing a place on a course. One trainee, who previously worked as a teaching assistant, said she had applied four times before being accepted,

I first applied after I had only had one year's experience working in schools. The tutors were very good at explaining the type of experience they thought I needed. My school was supportive and the head of my school was able to vary my opportunities to work in a variety of settings and with a range of children. It also gave me an opportunity to read more widely and meet EPs from my local service.

Interviews

As you might expect, each course has its own selection process but the trainees that we spoke with told us that they all included a personal interview, a written element and often a group activity of some sort. Details of all selection procedures can be found on each university website.

The interview was invariably with a tutor from the course and often an experienced EP associated with the course. Trainees said that the interview involved questions about previous experience, especially with children with special needs. They said they were also asked about their knowledge of current legislation concerning children and their opinions on the best way to support children and families. One question they were often asked was the extent to which psychology research and practice had helped them in their work with children. As one trainee told us:

> *During the day, we had two interviews: one academic and one about educational practice. In the academic interview, we responded to questions about any previous research experience we had had and were given the opportunity to talk about any interesting articles we had read. The focus in the practice interview was to share experiences of working with children and to reflect on the insights of psychology that might have helped us in our work.*

The group exercise in which some trainees had participated generally included a discussion about a hypothetical case in which the group had to discuss what they thought an EP might be able to contribute to achieving a positive outcome for a child or young person. Other group discussions included opinions on the role of EPs in the wider context of the education system and considered the value of cognitive assessment. At one programme, applicants were given a group task that involved a discussion about the different skills they thought an EP needed to develop.

Many programmes also included a written assignment. Some programmes expected this to be completed on the interview day, while other programmes required applicants to bring an assignment with them. Most trainees found this element of the selection process stressful. For one course the written assignment was based on a general discussion of the values of human rights legislation. On another course it was a research-based exercise, and on yet another course candidates were given a research paper to read and had to write their own individual abstracts for it. This type of exercise is an obvious attempt by the various universities to ascertain the ability of the candidates to formulate and set out an argument, to weigh up the pros and cons of an issue, and to quickly synthesise the key points of a paper. These all indicate essential skills that an EP needs, whether it is writing a report, an article for publication or conveying the key points of an argument or research. All the trainees we spoke to said that although, like any interview, it had been stressful, they all considered that they had been treated well. However, as we only spoke to those who had been successful it was unlikely they would have too many complaints! We will now turn our attention to an outline of the three years of training.

Year 1

All the trainees we spoke to found the first year of training very demanding indeed. They described the year as being 'content heavy'.

We were introduced to so many new concepts, issues and ideas, it was at times difficult to get your head around so much new information.

Several others pointed out that it had been several years since they had last been involved in serious study. This was especially the case for those who had a longer experience of working in schools; in one case the trainee who had ten years' experience in the classroom found the challenge especially demanding. However, all found the content of the course of immensely interesting.

It was extremely full. I learned so much about child development that I thought I already knew from university, but realise that I had just skimmed the surface before.

This was also the case in terms of what they learned about the value of child assessment. One trainee told us that up until she started training she had not appreciated the philosophical and ethical issues relating to assessment.

We had a series of workshops in which the issues of child-centred assessment, standardised assessment and dynamic assessment were fully explored. This proved extremely thought-provoking and has had a real impact on my thinking and practice.

Another taught part of the course comprises sessions on research methods and ethics. This is invaluable as trainees begin to write assignments and need to critically evaluate research, and as they begin to think about topics for the research that they will conduct in Years 2 and 3.

Many of the trainees commented that they had not appreciated the extent to which the work of an EP was bound up with legislation. Several told us that this section of the course was a real eye-opener, not only in terms of the limitations it places on the role of the EP, but also the extent to which an EP is, on one level, a local government officer (assuming that they are employed by a local authority and not working privately), which in itself opened up a whole set of philosophical issues about who is the client for an EP's work that they had not fully appreciated when they started training to become an EP.

Although it does vary between courses, invariably Year 1 also contains two field placements with a local EP service. The trainees were all positive about this experience. Students at one course reported that in the first term they visited a local service in small groups with their fieldwork supervisor and had the opportunity to work through a case as a group, which all found extremely helpful. The two longer placements were with services reasonably close to the university. Trainees pointed out that in both placements the local services were used to having trainees and had close working relationships with the course and their tutors. All the trainees said that during the placement they were expected to take responsibility for contributing to a number of active cases. They told us that these cases were selected to give them a balance of experience. They commented that they were able to discuss their cases with not only their personal tutor at the university, but that they also had considerable support from other members of the service who were always willing to provide it.

In addition to work with children and young people, trainees typically carry out project work or research during their first year. This might take the form of a small-scale research project aimed at following the research design process that will be used in the following year by a trainee in order to conduct their major research project. It will include experience of conducting research, collecting and analysing data, and writing up the findings in an academic style. You may well work in a group with other trainees, with the possibility of investigating something that is current in a local authority.

All the trainees told us that, throughout their time on the programme, the relationship they were able to build up with their personal tutor was the key to their success.

I met with my tutor every other week throughout the first year. I found this especially supportive, especially in being able to discuss the cases I was responsible for on the placement. He was also very useful to point me in the right direction when it came to written assignments and the preparation of my case file.

Most of the trainees commented that during the course of the first year the workload gradually increased and that, at times, they found it difficult to balance the demands of the written assignments, the preparation for various workshops and the case work they had been allocated on their placements, let alone the demands of family and relationships.

Year 2

The trainees we spoke to said that the experience they had had in the first year gave them a sound grounding for their second year. The main feature of the second year is placement in a local service. For most training programmes, the major difference from the first year placement is that trainees were expected to take on a proportionate caseload and, in most cases, they were given responsibility for providing a service to a specific group of schools. Usually they were gradually introduced to their schools but they all found the establishing of a working relationship with staff at times demanding but ultimately rewarding. One trainee told us that at the end of the year she had found it difficult to say goodbye. Another trainee spoke about the reasons why she had thoroughly enjoyed her placement in Year 2. She said that she likes

to feel part of a strong team and this has certainly been the case due to the ethos of the team I was with. I found that I shared many of their values and ways of working and this helped me to fit in very quickly.

She went on to say that she,

found it very helpful to be surrounded by a number of EPs who had also done the same training programme. This meant that they fully understood what expectations there were and were able to provide me with the experiences I needed to evidence over the year. The combination of their support and gentle challenges has helped me to grow in confidence and to reach a level of competence that seems miles away when you're in your first year!'

One or two trainees who only had experience of working in primary schools before starting training said they found it difficult at first to work with large secondary schools, especially with the demands of the separate learning support department and the pastoral team. Overall, though, a trainee should anticipate working in a variety of schools and settings:

I have been able to work in a range of different schools this year, including specialist settings and an independent school. The work carried out in these settings came with its own challenges and has helped me to think more deeply about the impact of the environment on the systems that operate around a child and their needs.

There are some targeted practice placements. For instance, trainees at Southampton are required to undertake a specialist diversity placement of nine days over three weeks. The purpose of this placement is for trainees to develop greater understanding of the influence of such factors as culture, gender, ethnicity and low socio-economic status, and implications for equality of opportunity and ethical practice.

The second year on some programmes can contain a lengthy written assignment. In the case of one trainee we spoke to, he told us that his assignment had been commissioned by the local authority he had been placed with.

They wanted to know more about the current prevalence of Autistic Spectrum Disorder (ASD). My assignment consisted of a thorough literature review. I was able to look at international, national and regional variations, including data I found out from the local health authority. The data I was able to collect was used by the authority to help plan future provision. I was made to feel that this was more than just an academic exercise but was valuable to the city as a whole. I was also asked to present the work at a regional conference, which was a very valuable experience.

Year 3

The final year of training for most trainees was dominated by the final placement and a research project that was written up as a thesis.

The second placement was described as similar to the first, but trainees were expected to take on more responsibility for their own work, especially in terms of management of their own diary, planning of work and reporting to schools. However, the final placement did give a number of trainees the opportunity to work in settings in which they were especially interested. One trainee told us that her interest lay in the future destinations of children in the care system and that, as a result, she had been given the opportunity to work in two children's homes within the local authority. She was also able to use the work she was doing with these young people as part of her research project.

In the third year trainees undertake a dissertation of 40,000–60,000 words. Many found this daunting at first but the process of developing their proposal gradually over the second year with support from their tutor made it more manageable. Also, because they had selected the title of their chosen subject in their second year, it had given them a chance to plan their work in stages. Course tutors had supported this process and, in a number of accounts, trainees had also received considerable help from other lecturers within their departments who had particular expertise in the trainee's area of study.

In this section we have attempted to summarise the experience of trainees during their training. As you might expect, the structure and organisation of each course is not identical. Each course has its own way of doing things, which may change over time. **When choosing a course you are advised to consult the website of each university for up-to-date information about course structure, organisation and content.**

Finance

Most of the trainees we spoke to had all survived the course without incurring massive debt. However, several had rescheduled their mortgage repayments but said that when they explained that they were training to their building society or bank, these organisations were sympathetic. The trainees that had previously been teaching assistants told us that they didn't experience any major change in standard of living. However, those that had previously been working as teachers or assistant educational psychologists said that they noticed the difference. One commented that she hadn't been able to buy any new clothes since she started training.

Course tutors will do their best to ensure that practical placements are convenient for a trainee and so are financially manageable. Travel expenses are reimbursed while carrying out placement work but other expenses are not. Unusually, one trainee said that on her course several of the placements had been some distance from the university. This meant that travel costs and some overnight stays had proved to be very expensive, especially for someone on a limited budget.

As we mentioned in the previous chapter, the funding for trainee EPs in Scotland is very different in that all trainees in Scotland were expected to self-fund their way on the course. As you might expect, this put added pressure on them. However, one trainee we spoke to said their tutors had been very helpful in pointing out the small number of scholarships available and how to apply for 'Professional Development Loans'. One trainee we spoke to said she had been seconded by her local authority. She told us:

> *I come from a small rural authority that has had problems recruiting EPs. When I asked our local EP for advice on qualifying, he arranged an interview with his boss, who agreed to second me if I promised to work locally in the future. Which wasn't a problem for me as I have always lived here.*

However, all the trainees we spoke to in their final year said that the financial sacrifice they had made had been worthwhile.

Last words

All the trainees we spoke to said that their training had been very thorough, stimulating and extremely rewarding. As one trainee said, speaking for most:

> *My favourite aspect of the programme is the practical element of it. I think it's fantastic that we get to experience first-hand what it is like to be an EP. Alongside this, there are various tutors and supervisors that we come into contact with throughout the three years. These are put in place by the university and this shows that they really value us as trainees and want us to succeed. I have also appreciated their attitude towards us as adult learners. Although there is a timetable in place, the EPs involved with the programme allow us to be flexible so that we can meet the requirements of the course in a way that suits us best. There are a range of different speakers provided for us each week, which means that we get to hear about a vast array of different topics that can be directly applied to our role as EPs. Alongside this, there is lots of encouragement to pursue topics that interest us so we can develop some more specialist knowledge.*

On the whole there is no doubt that the trainees that we spoke to had enjoyed their time on the course. Several, however, pointed out that it involved many demands, especially in terms of the volume of the work they were expected to produce. This was especially the case during their placements in Years 2 and 3, when they were given the responsibility of a caseload in addition to their other assignments. At the same time, being able to balance competing demands and make at times difficult judgments about priorities is important preparation for working as an EP without the safety net of a training programme.

Jonny Craig

Jonny gained his BSc psychology degree at Aston University in 2004. He almost became an accountant, but then received an offer to become a graduate researcher at Liverpool John Moores University (LJMU). While working there he became aware of the work of educational psychologists and applied for the doctorate course at Nottingham University.

His first job subsequent to completing the course was as an EP working with a Local Authority. Then, four years ago, together with colleague Dr David Lamb, he set up an independent Educational Psychology Service called 'Applied Psychologies'.

'We work with around 50 schools and settings across the North of England, mainly in Hull, north-east Lincolnshire, Lancashire and Liverpool. As well as a comprehensive Educational Psychology Service including assessment, intervention, staff training and therapeutic work, we now also offer an Autism Outreach Service.

We have also worked outside education, applying our experiences of working in schools with children and young people to Sports Psychology, supporting a number of young athletes to develop their skills.

We have now reached a stage where we employ a number of associate EPs and have recently recruited our first full-time Educational Psychologist. Establishing our service has given us more opportunities to develop creative ways of working.'

5 | Starting out

The aim of this chapter is to give you an idea of what to expect should and when you start your career as an EP. Life as a fully qualified EP is very different as you move from the 'cocooned' world of a university training course to becoming a fully-fledged autonomous practitioner. The first section will deal with the experience of trainees in securing their first job but the bulk of this chapter will deal with longer-term issues and your professional development.

Your first job as an EP is obviously extremely important to you. Virtually all job vacancies are posted on the website run by the Association of Educational Psychologists (AEP), although some jobs are also advertised on the *Times Educational Supplement* website and others through the British Psychological Society. Many of the trainees we spoke to had been appointed to a post with one of the Services in which they had had a placement as a trainee. This obviously has advantages in two ways. First, the trainee will have had an oppor-tunity to know and understand how that Service works and if it is a Service that they would like to work for and, second, the Service has an opportunity to get to know the strengths and development needs of their potential EP.

Our advice before you apply for any post is to learn as much as you can about the Service you are applying to join. You can do this in a number of ways. Ask around, especially the tutors on the training course and the EPs you have met on placement. As well as your own impressions of the Service in question, you may well know an EP in the Service who would be willing to talk with you informally and who can give you some inside information. Ensure that you carefully read the Service's website and relevant pages of the local authority's website to gain an idea of current policies and practices. Lastly, before any interview, it is good policy to ask to go on a visit to the Service to find out more about their culture and values, resources, facilities and funding, as well as information about caseloads, supervision and continuing professional development, organisation and policy.

Interviews for first jobs can be daunting. However, it is important to remember that as a new EP you are not expected to know everything. It is important that you are given an opportunity to tell the interview panel about the successes you have had as a trainee, how you have applied psychology theory, and your expectations for the future. It is essential that you are also given a chance to ask them questions about induction periods, supervision, professional development and opportunities for further research.

Once you have secured your first post there are many challenges ahead, some of which can have a major impact on your development as a professional and your effectiveness as a practitioner. While your training course will have exposed you to a wide range of experience, given you a thorough knowledge of many aspects of educational psychology and allowed you to explore some of these in depth, not least through your dissertation, invariably it cannot cover everything you need to know. The rest of this chapter will explain how to bridge that gap, increase your knowledge base, and begin to develop the skills you will need for a long and fulfilling career. It will also explain something of the role and function of the Health and Care Professionals Council (HCPC), which is the regulatory authority for psychologists working in this country.

The transition from trainee to fully fledged professional has been well described by Rosenberg (2014) 'Why support after training is important', available on: www.learningsolutionsmag.com/articles/1348/marc-my-words-the-training-to-competence-myth.

To a large extent the illustration (Figure 5.1) is self-explanatory. It shows the common assumption that training will provide all the necessary skills and competencies that any trainee will need in order to launch their career, but, as one recently qualified EP told us,

It's not until you start work that you realise how much you don't know!

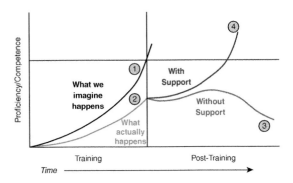

Figure 5.1   Maintenance of competencies after training

Life as a professional psychologist is one of continual learning. As our illustration shows, without a commitment to such learning our effectiveness as practitioners will diminish. More than that, all professional psychologists have a statutory obligation to continuing professional development, as is outlined in some depth by the HCPC.

Health and Care Professions Council

During your training you will hear about the Health and Care Professions Council or HCPC. This is an independent statutory body set up by the government essentially to protect the public. The HCPC regulates a range of professions, including educational psychologists. When you are fully qualified you will need to register as a 'practitioner psychologist' with the HCPC and pay a fee. 'Practitioner psychologist' is a legally protected title covering a number of different kinds of professional psychologists. The HCPC ensures that only fully qualified EPs are allowed to practice in the United Kingdom and that those that practice adhere to the highest professional standards. The HCPC publishes two sets of standards. There are Standards of Proficiency specifically for practitioner psychologists and Standards of Conduct, Performance and Ethics.

The HCPC expects trainee EPs to have full knowledge of these standards and abide by them during their training. The Standards of Conduct, Performance and Ethics apply to everyone registered with the HCPC; they are clear, unambiguous and cover all areas of an EP's work. A more detailed account of these standards can be found on the HCPC website.

You will have noted above that part of the remit of the HCPC is to ensure that EPs in the UK keep abreast of current research and developments in educational psychology and psychology in general. They are also expected to know about the latest developments in educational practice and of the effectiveness of various interventions. In order to ensure that registered members are keeping up to date a small number, usually about 5% of EPs, are selected each year to complete a detailed account of their professional development activities over the previous year. This includes a record of courses they may have attended, books and journals they have read, and other work they have undertaken to broaden or expand their knowledge and skills. There is also a section on how this increased knowledge or expertise has had an influence on their casework.

This process can take a number of days to complete. However, there are often other EPs in their Service who have completed a professional development audit previously and can give support.

Continuing professional development

Both the illustration from Rosenberg (2014; Figure 5.1) and the stipulation from the HCPC emphasise that all EPs have a duty to enhance and develop both their skills and knowledge. This process is called continuing professional development. It can cover a wide range of experiences but central to the process is the relationship the new EP creates with their supervisor. If you have not experienced supervision in a previous work role then as a trainee educational psychologist you will become familiar with the process in which all EPs meet with a fellow EP on a regular basis to discuss and review their work, discuss any issues or problems that have arisen since they last met, celebrate any successes and set short- or long-term goals. In addition to supervision, all EPs will have an annual appraisal or performance review, which should be with a senior or principal EP. This is another important opportunity to set out development goals for the following year, as well as to review other aspects of practice.

Supervision policies vary across different Services but generally supervision should be relatively frequent during the induction period, gradually moving to at least a monthly meeting. Supervision includes a number of elements all of which can add to an EP's effectiveness and aid their development. These elements are listed below.

Learn to reflect on yourself and your service delivery

Reflection is a central element of any supervision process and involves thinking about your experiences and asking yourself, what have I learned from this case? What did I do well? What might I have done better? What might I do differently next time? In supervision more time tends to be spent dealing with problem cases and situations but it is also important to spend time looking at successes and analysing what it was about that particular case that led to a successful outcome. The role of your supervisor is very important here, especially when you start out, as he or she will have considerable experience and will be able to guide you.

Learning from your clients

As an EP you have a number of 'clients'; children and young people, parents, teachers, schools and the local authority or Service for which you work. As such it is important to always seek feedback from all individuals and groups on what they think about your involvement and its effectiveness. As one recently qualified EP told us,

> *My training was very child-centred. We were encouraged to ensure that the child or young person was happy to work with us. I always ask the young person I see how they feel about working with me and if they are happy with the things I suggest.*

Parents are also a very perceptive source of feedback and will often be the first to tell you how their child has progressed following any intervention. Unlike teachers, who often report back in terms of changes in attitude to learning, learning progress or changes in behaviour, parents inevitably will focus in terms of their child's happiness or well-being.

The feedback we get from schools can be more formal. Some local authorities conduct annual surveys about the performance of support services, which can include EP services. However, in terms of the newly qualified EP, feedback from schools is best achieved personally. One new EP told us,

> *I was encouraged by my supervisor to always make sure the last person I talked to when I was leaving the school was the Head Teacher. I always make a point of informing him or her what I have done, why I have taken this particular approach and what I hope will be the outcome. In short, I make sure they are happy with what I have done. In my experience this approach has been very useful to me. Heads have considerable experience and will be the first to tell me when I am on the right track, or if I need to consider other avenues.*

Learn from your supervisor

> *My supervisor has been great. She has been so supportive to me, not only in terms of her knowledge about the way that the local services work but also in a wider range of issues. She has been very open with me and introduced me to a number of approaches that I had only heard about but never seen in action. She gave me a lot of confidence in knowing that I was doing the right sort of things and was very supportive over one particular difficult case.*

This type of reaction was typical of a number of newly qualified EPs to whom we talked. No EP, however experienced, can expect all cases to go well. An experienced supervisor will be able to take a long-term view of your development and is in a position to point you in a direction where you can enhance your experience and expertise. In this respect they have a very important role in enhancing your development by suggesting further reading, attendance at courses and possible research.

Learning from colleagues

As we have seen, most EPs work in teams and therefore share offices, meet regularly and invariably share experiences, both of their successes and of their failures. Colleagues can be a tremendous support to newly qualified EPs. As one recently qualified EP told us,

> *When I started out I shared an office with an established EP. She had a lot of experience working with difficult families. Whenever I had a difficult case I always asked her for advice. She was a great help and on a number of cases we worked jointly, visiting the family together. She taught me so much.*

Learning from the literature

As a professional EP you have an obligation to keep abreast of recent research and developments in the field of educational psychology. Educational psychologists also keep up to date through reading journals and books. The main journals read by EPs in the UK are *Educational Psychology in Practice* and *Educational and Child Psychology*. Both these journals are published quarterly and contain articles written by practicing EPs, encompassing a wide range of topics and subjects. There are also a number of journals aimed at an international audience, for example *School Psychology International*, or at areas of special education such as autism. A number of educational psychology services take keeping up with journals seriously and organise a 'Journal Club', which meets every half-term and each club member talks about one recent paper that has caught their eye.

Learning through attending courses

Attending a national course or conference is a very effective way of keeping up to date. There are regular courses arranged for EPs. Both the Association of Educational Psychologists (AEP) and the division of the British Psychological Society for EPs, the Division of Educational and Child Psychologists (DECP), run annual courses specifically aimed at updating EPs' knowledge and skills. A number of universities also run their own independent courses, for instance University College London organises an annual 'leading edge' day for this purpose. There are also regional courses and those provided for special interest groups such as the National Autistic Society.

Educational Psychology Services themselves will also run their own courses or conferences, which are often open to neighbouring services and others in the local authority. Naturally, a course is not the only way of developing knowledge and practice. For example, one of the authors works in a Service that organises an annual day where a team spends a morning in a local school practising dynamic assessment and then part of the afternoon both reflecting on and discussing developments in practice.

Learning through your own research

One of the most important elements of your training to become an EP will be your dissertation. The aim of the dissertation is both to develop an in-depth knowledge of one specific area of educational psychology and also to train you in research methodology and analysis. Research has always been an important element in EPs' lives. Many EP Services encourage members to engage in research and evaluation, often as a method of examining the effectiveness of either their Service or perhaps the effectiveness of a specific specialist unit or intervention. In fact, a number of recently trained EPs used their doctoral thesis as a basis to publish their research to a wider audience. As one told us,

> *My doctoral study was on the effectiveness of a teacher training programme called Assertive Discipline. I wanted to see whether the programme had an effect on the children's engagement in lessons, but also on their enjoyment. Both my tutor at university and my supervisor encouraged me to publish the results. I'm glad to say it was published by* Educational Psychology in Practice.

Membership of professional organisations

We have already mentioned the two professional organisations that serve the needs of educational psychologists, The Association of Educational Psychologists (AEP) and the British Psychological Society (BPS), in terms of their publications and courses. Both provide support for EPs but in different ways. Most EPs are a member of at least one of these organisations and we would encourage any qualified EP to do the same.

Association of Educational Psychologists (AEP)

The AEP is both the professional organisation of EPs and also their trade union. At present over 80% of all educational psychologists in England, Northern Ireland and Wales are members of the AEP. You can join the AEP as a trainee educational psychologist at a reduced rate.

As an AEP member you are part of a trade union, which gives you a degree of protection, should you require it, if there are any difficulties with your employers, whether they be a local authority or a private company. The AEP negotiates on rates of pay and terms and conditions of service with the employers at a national level through the Soulbury Committee.

On a professional level the AEP is responsible for the publication of *Educational Psychology in Practice* (*EPiP*). This journal is the most widely read and most widely distributed journal for EPs in this country. It receives submissions from EPs from all over the world, but the majority of published articles are from practicing EPs in the UK. As we mentioned previously, the AEP organise an annual course on which EPs can hear about the latest research from other EPs, allied professions, university-based researchers and government spokespersons. The AEP also organise regional and local area meetings.

As members, EPs have access to the AEP website, which contains useful information, contacts and a 'job vacancies' section. Every week members of the AEP are emailed with a news and information update and, separately, the latest job vacancies from England and Wales.

The world of work for EPs is ever-changing and therefore, we would argue, it is important to have some sort of protection that being a member of a union affords you. Whether you choose to join the AEP or not is your option but almost all working EPs are members, which speaks volumes for its credibility and influence.

British Psychological Society, Division of Educational and Child Psychology

As a holder of a psychology degree you are entitled to become a member of the British Psychology Society (BPS). Currently the BPS has over 50,000 members and is hugely influential in all matters to do with all branches of psychology in the United Kingdom. This is the learned society for all psychologists that, among other things, aims to promote and advance psychology as a discipline, to be the authoritative and public voice of psychology, and to assure the highest standards. As a member of the BPS you receive a copy of a monthly magazine called *The Psychologist*. This magazine has articles on all areas of psychology from sport to the arts, book and film reviews, as well as more informative in-depth articles on all aspects of our science. It also has some job adverts, but not many specifically aimed at EPs.

The BPS also has various special groups, sections and divisions representing different scientific and professional interests. As a member of the BPS you can apply to become a member of the Division of Educational and Child Psychologists (DECP). You will probably come across the DECP during your training as they run an annual course for trainee EPs, which is usually well attended and is an opportunity for trainees learn about recent research, present their work to each other and, of course, to socialise. The trainee conference is usually held the day before the DECP annual conference, an event at which a wide variety of workshops and papers are presented by EPs and others to disseminate their work and good practice. This conference often attracts a small number of delegates from abroad and is an opportunity to meet fellow EPs from all over the country.

The DECP is also responsible for the publication of two journals of interest to EPs. The first is called *Educational and Child Psychology*. It comes out four times a year. Each edition covers a specific theme and it is a good way of keeping up to date with the latest trends in educational psychology and of broadening your knowledge. The DECP also publishes a less formal publication called *Debate*. *Debate* is a lively collection of short articles, letters from members, book reviews and news of the DECP. It is another good way of learning what other EPs in the country are doing.

Membership of both the AEP and DECP are extremely important for every EP. In both their ways they represent the profession to the country and to government and provide, through their journals and conferences, the opportunities for our profession to improve and develop.

Ethics and values

In the earliest stages of training you will be introduced to the ethics and values of the profession. This is because all EPs have to adhere to strict ethical principles, which are outlined in the HCPC documentation and enshrined in the principles of both the BPS and the AEP. The principles have their basis in the United Nations Convention on the Rights of the Child (UNCRC, 1989), which place the child as our primary client and bind us to always put their needs before all others.

The work of EPs is strongly driven by the values of human rights and inclusive practices and EPs are not afraid of controversy. A director of education in a large north-eastern city once described EPs as 'the conscience of the local authority' because of the willingness of EPs to question accepted practice. In 1970 EPs were the subject of controversy themselves, when Bernard Coard highlighted the disproportionate representation of African-Caribbean children in what were then called schools for the educationally subnormal. This was due to the use of IQ tests, with inherent cultural and class bias, which also took no account of the cultural and emotional upheaval many of these children had experienced in moving from the West Indies to the UK. It is telling, though, that EPs themselves were members of the Caribbean Education and Community Worker's Association that published Coard's pamphlet. In 1975, Margaret Dubberley, an EP working in Sheffield, successfully brought legal proceedings to prevent the sterilisation of an 11-year-old girl who was attending a special school that Margaret worked with. In the early 1980s, one of the authors of this book was among a group of EPs at the forefront of a campaign to abolish corporal punishment, including writing a booklet for the Association of Educational Psychologists on *Alternatives to Corporal Punishment*. In addition to the same kind of human rights perspective that motivated Margaret, psychological evidence shows that corporal punishment cannot affect the behaviour it is intended to punish and stop.

A common ethical issue that faces EPs relates to demands for a 'quick fix', either in response to a sense of crisis or to avoid using too much EP time. This often occurs because of the influence of what is termed 'the medical model', with its perspective that there is something wrong within an individual child or young person that can be diagnosed and cured, often by medication. For example, a number of EPs have raised concerns about the number of British children who have been given medication in response to a diagnosis of 'attention deficit hyperactivity disorder' (ADHD). In their view, too many children were being given medication as a quick fix to change their behaviour rather than using behavioural techniques, which are potentially more effective but might take longer and require more effort to implement. They have organised conferences to make all EPs aware of the issue and have lobbied parliament to bring it to the attention of MPs. Diagnostic labels in themselves can be ethically problematic, particularly when their widespread use leads to emotive reactions rather than rational ones. As we mentioned earlier, the use of the label 'dyslexia' has been challenged on the basis of a thorough review of research evidence. This has led to the conclusion that 'dyslexia', as a label, lacks an agreed coherent description with no consensus on a coherent strategy of how to ameliorate the problem.

Concluding remarks

Starting off in any new job can be stressful, although the experience of working under supervised practice as a trainee EP will have given you a good sense of what to expect. As a new EP you will have to learn new procedures and ways of working, quickly establish working relationships and get to know a new set of work colleagues. However, in our experience, EPs are more than willing to support new colleagues both formally and informally as they make their way in the profession. The level of job satisfaction among EPs is high. Most enjoy their work although it can be demanding at times. However, as we will learn in the following chapter, being an EP can lead to very interesting careers both within the profession and outside.

Dan Small

Dan studied psychology at Leeds Metropolitan University. He worked as a Teaching Assistant at a local secondary school in Formby and then at an independent special school for children with Social, Emotional and Behavioural Difficulties (SEBD).

'Initially I was just interested in working in Education, but while at Formby High the Senco told me about the role of Educational Psychologists and that type of work appealed to me. While working at the special school I saw a job as a Psychology Assistant in Buckinghamshire working with the Educational Psychology Service. This job included some intervention work as well as helping the Authority with some research on Nurture Groups.'

Dan then earned a place on the Newcastle training course, where his thesis was on 'Teacher Well-Being'. He now works for the West Cheshire and Chester Education Authority.

A career in educational psychology

As we learned in the last chapter, EPs can expect to start off as a main grade EP, working with a group of schools. It is possible that their responsibilities also include some specialist work such as working in units or schools for children and young people with special educational needs. Most EPs also find themselves working with pre-school children.

This type of work can provide a high degree of job satisfaction but, as their experience grows, most EPs will want to extend their experience and begin to develop a degree of specialisation in an area that interests them. Invariably, as part of their supervision, an EP will have discussed their interests with their manager, usually a Senior EP. Also, as part of their appraisal or annual review, they will have an opportunity to discuss their longer-term goals and ambitions with their Senior EP or Principal. As you might expect, any special interest they might have has to be compatible with the needs of the service but, as EPs are involved with such a wide range of work, there are invariably opportunities for an EP to be allocated an area of responsibility in which they can develop their interest.

Pay

The vast majority of EPs in this country are paid on the Soulbury Pay Scales. The Soulbury Committee meets annually and is a collective bargaining forum for negotiating the salaries and terms and conditions of service for local authority educational advisory professionals. Scale A is for main grade EPs. An EP is paid on four consecutive points of the scale and these four points can vary by local authority. However, as an EP gains more experience and expertise, they might expect that this would be reflected in the salary. In fact this is the case, as there are what are called 'Structured Professional Assessment' (SPA) points at the top of the scale and any EP can apply to be considered for an increase in salary. At the time of writing the span of remuneration for Scale A is between £35,731 to £49,810, but a successful application for additional SPA can raise this further up to £52,903. All up-to-date pay scales are available on the AEP website.

As we indicated in Chapter 2, while most EPs in the majority of services are employed directly by their local authority on a salaried basis, this is not the case with all areas. In some areas, although the Psychological Service does directly employ a number of EPs, much of the work with schools is carried out by Associate EPs. These are self-employed and paid on a contractual basis by individual schools. Thus, the school can negotiate with the EP over the type and nature of the service they require. We have spoken with a number of these Associates and they told us about the advantages of their role. They are employed directly by the schools in which they work. They tend to be contracted to work so many days a year in the school, which gives them an opportunity to develop more preventative-type approaches. They do not get involved in statutory work. On the downside, they told us that they are responsible for their own administrative work and have to organise their own tax and pension arrangements.

Senior Educational Psychologists

Most local authority services have a leadership structure that includes the post of Senior Educational Psychologist (SEP). In many cases these posts carry responsibility for managing a section of the Psychological Service and, especially in some of the large English counties, a team of EPs will be led by a SEP, who will in turn be responsible to the Principal EP.

In other services there may be senior posts mainly to lead and manage specialist functions, such as organising the service to pre-school children, working with groups of special schools, organising clinics for children who may be on the Autistic Spectrum, or managing EP professional development, and research and evaluation. Until recently, one EP service had a senior EP who managed a research and evaluation unit that employed a number of research psychologists. Invariably all SEP posts are advertised nationally and therefore are open for any qualified and experienced EP to apply. As you might expect, both SEP and Principal Educational Psychologists are paid at a higher rate than other EPs. They are paid on what is called Soulbury Scale B. Like main grade EPs, they too can apply for additional discretionary pay through 'Structured Professional Assessment' points, which reflect both experience and specialisation.

Principal Educational Psychologists

All local authority psychological services are led by a Principal Educational Psychologist (PEP). In some cases the job title may be slightly different, but the profession as a whole has always insisted that any service is led by a qualified EP. This is a very important issue, especially in light of the statutory regulation of the profession. Because of the complex nature of an EP's role, a qualified EP as a principal has the insight into all aspects of the work, is able to support other EPs over difficult or contentious issues and cases, and provides them with the professional leadership any service requires.

Unlike EPs and SEPs, who spend the majority of their time in schools, seeing children and parents, and discussing programmes with teachers, inevitably PEP spend less of their time on these types of activities as they adopt a leadership role. Such a role has its own share of challenges and is often extremely demanding. It does, however, give a chance for the PEP to act as an essential voice and representative of the value of educational psychology and EPs, and also to have an influence over such things as local authority strategy and practice developments. As one PEP told us,

I think it is important that psychology has a voice within the Education Service. I think our psychological skills have often been underestimated. Within my own authority I have been able to have input into the way we evaluate initiatives, which is a skill that I developed while studying for my doctorate.

Often PEPs end up being responsible for not only the Psychological Service but also other local authority services, such as Behavioural Support Teams, Early Years Assessment Teams or School Attendance Teams.

Another PEP related how, shortly after been appointed, the nature of her job began to change:

> *When I was appointed, I was only responsible for the running of the Educational Psychology Service (EPS). However, my Authority decided to form a Schools Support Service. This comprised Educational Advisors and Attendance Officers and the Early Years Advisory Team. I was flattered to be invited to lead the new team. We have been able to initiate some very innovative ways of working, including joint working on attendance issues, and on school improvement. This school improvement work has helped some schools that were deemed to be failing and in 'Special Measures' to turn around and become successful again. I think the advisors learnt a lot from the EPs about how to improve learning and behaviour and EPs learned a great deal about the dimensions of how schools work.*

Developing expertise

Most EPs can expect to spend a considerable proportion of their careers as main grade EPs. During this time they will inevitably come across a wide range of issues that are having an impact on the lives of children. In response to these issues EPs develop a wide range of skills and expertise to meet these demands. These skills are acquired by working alongside experienced colleagues, by reading widely in journals and books, and often by attending specialised training opportunities. In the following section we will give a number of examples of some of the techniques and approaches that EPs have developed and refined for their work with children. The examples we have chosen are an attempt to give you a flavour of the wide range of skills that are used by EPs across the country, and to give you some idea of the type of work you will encounter should you eventually become an EP.

Strategies to help children's learning

Paired reading

Paired reading is a simple technique that has been used to help children's reading skills. It was originally pioneered by an EP called Roger Morgan and has, since then, been used extensively in all types of schools.

The technique is deceptively easy. In the initial phase the child and the tutor, usually a teacher, teaching assistant or parent, read out loud simultaneously. If the child can't read the word or reads it incorrectly the tutor merely says the word correctly and they move on. The tutor has to adjust their speed of reading to that of the child. As the child gains in confidence, the adult can phase out their support by gradually reducing their volume or the child can indicate that they want to read alone by nudging the tutor. The tutor only joins in again if the child reaches a word they cannot read.

Paired reading as an approach has a number of advantages. First, it can be used with any type of reading material. A good example of this was when one of the authors of this book (Jeremy Swinson) was working in Liverpool. He was asked to help a boy aged eleven who had a reading age of under seven. The boy's father explained that his son was fed up with reading what he thought were 'baby books'. It transpired that both father and son were huge Everton fans and that the young boy always wanted to have a look at the 'Everton pages' of the local evening paper, the *Liverpool Echo*, when his dad brought it home each night. The EP then explained and demonstrated the paired reading technique to both of them together and it was agreed that they would read about their team every single night. This intervention proved a great success as the boy's reading age improved by more than three years over the next nine months.

The second major advantage of the technique is that it is comparatively easy to learn to do. As a result, a number of EPs have devised schemes for teaching groups of parents from the schools they work with to use the method with their own children. It has also been found to be very easy to teach children to become tutors. One recently qualified EP called Emma told us:

I learned about paired reading on my course and began suggesting that it was used by both parents and teaching assistants in one of my schools. The head teacher of the school suggested we use the approach in a 'Reading Buddy' scheme she had already used in another school, where more able readers in Year 6 were paired up with less confident readers from Years 4 and 5. I found a training pack to train peer readers which I used to train ten older pupils. Once trained they were given a certificate and allocated a younger pupil to work with. I was able to evaluate the project and found it was a great success, not only in improving the reading skills of the less confident readers but also their self-esteem and that of their older tutors.

Precision Teaching

Precision Teaching (PT) is a technique that has been pioneered by EPs in this country for some time. It is based on the ideas of a psychologist called Lev Vygotsky. He pointed out the obvious, which is that children's learning takes place gradually and that effective teaching should be geared towards a learner's 'zone of proximal development' (ZPD). Precision Teaching encourages teachers to be very specific about the materials they use with the child, to practise the skills on a daily basis and to monitor progress every week. As Tony, an experienced EP, told us:

I have been using PT for some years. Over the years I have acquired a lot of material, including a number of 'probes' which help me gauge the child's level of understanding. I like the way PT shows us how a child needs to be fluent in new learning before it can be maintained effectively. When we use the technique, I use one my 'probes' to work out the child's current level of skill. We then work together to set targets. The teacher or teaching assistant then spends 5 to 10 minutes teaching the child two new items using whatever teaching method they think is best. We then see how many times they can get it right in a minute. The teacher logs correct items and errors so that a target is set for the next round. These are then recoded on a chart.

Tony told us that he has used the technique in both primary and secondary schools and found it to be especially effective in basic skills, such as reading and spelling, but he has also used it to help young people with problems in maths. Precision Teaching has proved to be very effective because of the precise monitoring of the child's learning. It means that you can focus very closely on exactly which material a child is struggling with, which methods are proving effective, and it tells you when a child has achieved a level of fluency with their new learning, which reduces the likelihood of learning being 'lost'.

Strategies to help children's emotional and social development

Cognitive Behavioural Therapy

Cognitive Behavioural Therapy (CBT) is a therapeutic approach that is used widely with adults in a range of settings to help deal with issues such as depression, anxiety or problematic behaviours such as gambling addiction. Although originally developed with adults, it is now widely used with children and young people. Unlike many therapeutic approaches, it is very much focussed on developing coping strategies to solve current behavioural problems or issues. Cognitive Behavioural Therapy uses a staged approach to help the individual identify the critical behaviours that are giving rise to problems, and to discuss practical ways in which these behaviours could be decreased or eliminated. Cognitive Behavioural Therapy works on the premise that our thoughts, feelings, emotions, beliefs and behaviours are all interrelated and, by attempting to modify these, we can change behaviour. Garry Squires, an EP based at Manchester University, has used this approach extensively with secondary pupils to help them improve their self-control and behaviour in school. An EP from Hampshire also used it at a secondary school to help a group of 19 girls whose teachers thought they would benefit from accessing an intervention to reduce anxiety. The girls were allocated into groups and the EP, together with a teaching assistant, worked with the group for six sessions. The sessions proved very successful, both in terms of reduced anxiety measures used by the EP, but also because all the girls reported that they found the sessions very helpful indeed and they had helped them to reduce worry. The parents of the girls were also asked how they thought that their daughters had got on and they said they were favourably impressed.

There is very strong evidence to show that CBT is a very effective way of helping children and young people improve their learning and behaviour.

Video Self-Modelling

Video Self-Modelling (VSM) is a technique that has been used in psychology for some time, but since modern mobile phones all have a video facility it has become much more widely used by EPs. Video Self-Modelling is a form of observational learning in which individuals observe themselves performing a behaviour successfully on video and then imitate the targeted behaviour. The theoretical basis of VSM comes from Professor Albert Bandura's work on social learning theory. His research showed that children can acquire skills by observing other people performing those skills, as well as through personal experience. Video Self-Modelling has been used successfully to help in a number of settings, but especially in helping children who exhibit selective mutism. These are children who, although they often speak normally at home, don't speak in school. The condition has been found in a number of children known to be on the Autistic Spectrum, but this is not always the case. Karen, an experienced EP, told us how she used the technique in such a case:

James was six and had been diagnosed with Autism Spectrum Disorder (ASD) and was selectively mute in school. During his reception year he had started to speak a little but, after the summer holidays in Year 1, this progress had been reversed. He displayed much anxiety in school and did not interact with other children, except at playtimes when he played football with the other boys. I arranged a meeting in school with his mother to discuss the issues and suggested that VSM might be a way to help deal with the problem. We invited James into the meeting and explained how we wanted to help him. He gave his consent with a nod. His mother said that she would ask him to make a video at home. Next day he brought his mother's phone into school with a video of him saying 'Hello my name is James and this is me talking'. He showed it to his teacher. This was the first time she had heard him speak. Next, in school, together with the SENCO, he made

a slightly longer video saying 'Hello' and naming his favourite foot-
ball team. He then showed this to his teacher and his class mates on
his table. The following week he made a video of himself saying 'Good
morning Mrs McGeehan', and followed this by saying the same phrase
when his name was called in registration. This was the first time he
had done this. Also in this week, he asked his teacher for a drink. In
the third week, each table of children in the class was asked to suggest
three places they would like to visit and tell the rest of the class. The
teacher suggested that all groups record their suggestions on a short
video, which was then presented to the rest of the class. James, with the
SENCO's help, joined in with the activity and said a short sentence.
During that week his teacher noticed that he had begun talking to the
others on his table and also volunteered to answer a question in class.

Karen went on to say that she thought that VSM worked on a number of levels, in that it allows the child in the first instance to practise
what they are going to say so there is less fear of failure, but also that it
allows individuals to see themselves as successful and gives them confidence. Video Self-Modelling has been used in a number of settings by
EPs, including helping teachers to improve their teaching and in aiding
young people with severe learning issues to gain new skills.

Other approaches to selective mutism

Video Self-Modelling is not the only approach that an EP might use to
help non-talkers. One of the authors of this book (Jeremy Swinson) was
referred a selective mute. He suggested VSM might be helpful, but the
young man in this case declined the offer so a more pragmatic approach
was used.

The child, BJ, was 10 years old and in Year 5 of a junior school. He
did not speak in infant school or for the first two years in his junior
school. According to his parents, he did speak at home. School staff
had noticed that he had been heard to speak at break times to one other
pupil and that he had spoken to Mrs P, the school secretary. He had
been referred to the CAMHs team and had attended two sessions, but
he had refused to speak to them so the referral was, in the words of his
mother, 'a complete waste of time'.

A meeting with the parents, the school's SENCO, and the class teacher was arranged. The parents were keen for BJ to talk in school, especially as secondary transfer was not too far away. In discussion it was discovered that, on a school holiday the previous week, BJ had in fact talked to an instructor as part of an activity, he had also talked outside in the playground and was happy to talk to Mrs P. The use of VSM was proposed but BJ did not think it was a good idea. However, he did agree that he needed to talk more in school and with his teacher Mrs C, as she needed to hear him read in order to evaluate his skills.

A plan was devised in which he would gradually talk to more adults and pupils every week. A key principle was that every week he would have to do something new. At the end of the meeting he met with his parents, the class teacher and myself, we outlined the programme and BJ agreed to 'have a go'.

In week 1 he agreed to read out loud to a fellow pupil (EH) in the corridor outside class, he would take a message to Mrs P and bring a message back, and he would be asked a simple direct question in a small social communication group. At the end of this week he had achieved all goals. Furthermore, the message from Mrs P was not a single word but involved telling the teacher what choices were available from a take-out menu.

In week 2 he read out loud to more pupils and to his teacher, Mrs C. She encouraged him to take messages to all members of staff and to bring back replies. He also contributed to a small group discussion in a social communication group and was videoed in drama group, which was later shown to all the class. At the end of the week he was able to ask all members of staff for their menu choices and report these back to his teacher. His contribution to class discussion was limited to very simple sentences, but he did talk.

On return from half-term, the weekly goals were set by the class teacher. Each day he was set a task that involved interacting with both staff and pupils. At a meeting in school on week 4, it was reported that he had delivered 'World Book Day' vouchers with a message to every member of staff, spoken to two classroom assistants for the first time, talked to people at Lancaster University on a school trip, and in class he joined in with repeating lines in French from a playscript. His maths teacher reported that, for the first time, he was putting up his hand and asking for help with problems.

The following week it was planned for him to rehearse lines from a play with his classroom assistant. Towards the end of term the play was to be videoed and shown to the rest of the school. He was also set the task of singing in church with the rest of his class at the Easter service. At this point it was decided at a meeting with his mother that the EP didn't need to be involved anymore. The school agreed to monitor BJ's behaviour and consult the Psychology Service if there were any problems, especially concerning secondary transfer.

His class teacher Mrs C said that over the course of four school weeks BJ had gained the confidence to talk to all adults in school, he was beginning to converse more with his peers, to ask teachers for help and to answer questions in class. This outcome was in sharp contrast to previous efforts to encourage him to talk. A great deal of the success of this intervention was due to Mrs C, who quickly understood the message 'a new challenge every day', and had the skill and confidence to work with BJ to achieve this. This is a good example of the ways in which EPs can empower teachers to have the confidence to try new and innovative approaches. His parents are delighted with the outcome.

Exam stress

We all find exams stressful. An EP called Dave Putwain, now at Liverpool John Moores University, has carried out extensive research in this area. He found that those pupils with special educational needs are particularly vulnerable to exam stress and that what he calls 'fear' appeals (for example, predicted dire consequences for not doing well) and negative feedback were more likely to have a harmful effect on a pupil's motivation and success. Conversely, he found that teachers that were perceived to be caring, fair, had high expectations but were supportive in helping pupils in terms of subject knowledge and engaging them in meaningful activities, were thought by the pupils to be helpful in supporting them through the exam process. A number of EPs have become interested in supporting students with exam stress and as one, Deborah, told us:

I was originally asked to see just one girl in Year 11 just prior to her GCSEs. I was able to help her with some relaxation techniques but, having read more extensively about the research in this area,

I suggested to the head of Year 11 that the following year I should begin working with any potential problems in September. This was arranged. The head of year together with the SENCO suggested seven young people in the year who might benefit from such an approach. The group met every month and worked on not only issues like relaxation, but also on building up confidence and self-esteem, revision techniques and planning, and supporting one another. The young people told me they really enjoyed the sessions and thought that it benefitted them when the exams eventually came around.

The success of the intervention was discussed by the senior management of the school, who then asked me to run a series of workshops for the whole staff. It did surprise me how one intervention with one girl can lead to a whole-school project. It showed me the importance of research and why it is so necessary to develop your skills.

Critical incidents

In recent years EPs have developed expertise in helping schools respond to major incidents that can have considerable impact on the lives of children in the school. Although some of these major incidents receive extensive publicity, such as the Hillsborough disaster or the fire at Grenfell Tower, there are a number of smaller events in the life of schools for which the school needs advice and support. As Mary, a very experienced EP, told us:

In our service, we quickly saw the need for all EPs in the county to be trained in critical incident work. We found ourselves responding to a variety of episodes in which schools asked us to become involved. In our area, there are many service families. As a result, the death of a parent often receives considerable publicity, which is not always helpful to the child. We have also been asked for advice when a teacher died in front of a class. As you can imagine, this one incident proved very challenging for the school, teachers, pupils and the EPs.

At these times, the critical incident team suspend all other work and devote all their time to the one school. We do not offer counselling to the children, but we offer a range of advice and support to the school, from guidance to the teachers on how to discuss the issues

*with their pupils to suggestions to the head teachers on the best way
to handle the press.*

*We always work in pairs on this type of work. It can be demanding
at times, but the feedback we get from schools is very positive.*

We also spoke to a number of other psychologists involved in critical
incident teams. They all explained that such work has to be well planned
and that it is important that when the team is set up, as many schools
as possible are trained to respond to such a situation. The teams all produce a booklet for schools explaining best practice, and they explain to
the schools that their team will respond to any incident within 24 hours
and will be able to devote as much time to the school as they need.

Strategies to help with school attendance

Dealing with attendance

Educational psychologists don't usually get involved with wider
attendance issues in schools; this was once generally the dedicated
role of Education Welfare Officers (EWO). With the reduction in
local authority budgets, many Education Welfare Services have disap-
peared. Sometimes they have been absorbed into other services set up
to offer early intervention with vulnerable children and young people,
or dealing with non-attendance has become part of the role carried
out by practitioners attached to a school, such as learning mentors
or home–school link workers. However, EPs can be called in to deal
with complicated cases or where other approaches have failed. In these
cases, it is important that the EP conducts a thorough and detailed case
history to help determine the causes of the problem and hence choose
the appropriate strategy for helping the young person. This is a very
important step, because it is essential to differentiate between what
were traditionally called 'school phobics' and those who are classified
as 'school refusers'. Generally, the distinction is now made between
'emotionally based school refusal' and those children whose school
refusal is due to truancy, often without the knowledge of their parents
or where parents have condoned the truancy. In the main, EPs do not
get involved in cases of truancy unless there are underlying emotional

reasons. There are two broad approaches used for those children show-ing emotionally based school refusal.

The first approach was developed by an EP called Nigel Blagg and invariably requires EPs to work in a team, either with other EPs or with Education Welfare Officers (EWO), teachers from the pupil's school or other practitioners. Once the pupil has been referred by the school, the EP gathers information from the school and visits the family at home, often with a colleague, to make sure this is a suitable case. The EP explains to the child and family that staying at home is not an option and that they will work with the family to help the pupil return to school. Often it is agreed that the pupil can go into a class with their favourite teacher or spend playtime with a friend, but invariably it is agreed that the pupil has to attend school all day. The EP then liaises with the school and a date is agreed for the pupil's return. On the morning in question, before the start of school, the EP and a colleague arrives at the home to help support the family to get the pupil out of the house and to the school. Often the EP or another worker will offer to drive the pupil and parent to school on the first day. This initial return to school can often be very difficult but it is important for the family and the EP to work together to ensure attendance. Once the team has got the pupil into school on day one it is important that, for the rest of the week, the fam-ily is supported by a team member every morning. The success rate of this technique is very high. One recently qualified EP, Jim, told us of his experience of using this approach:

> *I discussed these cases with my supervisor. He told me about Nigel's work. His technique is a sort of immersion approach, and the opposite of what you might expect. It's not, then, a gradual approach where you encourage the young person to visit the school for a brief period and then encourage them to successively increase the amount of time they spend in school. In one particular case, once the problem had been fully discussed with teachers and parents, a date was set for a return to school. I set up a team, which included myself and the EWO and a behavioural support worker from the school. We set up a rota so the family had a visit every morning for the first 10 days of the plan. Once a date has been fixed, I promised that a member of the team will arrive at their house at 8:15 every morning for a week in order to assist the parents getting the young person into school. On the first*

day the EWO and myself visited the home. Everyone was on edge and at first the pupil was reluctant to cooperate. However, we were able to persuade him to leave the house. On the first day, I gave the family a lift in my car, but once the young person has attended you find that the family rely on their own resources.

Jim told us that this approach, although time-consuming at first, actually paid dividends in the long term because it empowered the parents in particular and supported them to become much more assertive in their relationship with their child. He said that although the technique was not appropriate for all cases, he found it to be very successful in a number of schools on his 'patch'. He therefore wrote up an account of his work for his colleagues, who then discussed it at one of their monthly meetings. As a result, he was able to act to support a number of his colleagues whenever a similar case arose in their schools. He told us that this type of intensive support had also been adopted by two of the schools he worked with and he had been asked to train a number of Educational Welfare Officers (EWO) who are specifically responsible for school attendance.

Another approach EPs use is very different. Again, it is important to gain a full history and find out from the pupil, family and school why the child finds going to school so stressful. Often emotionally based school refusal develops gradually over time and is evident from an increasingly irregular attendance pattern. On speaking to the child, he or she may be able to explain their anxieties and fears. At this point the EP could do two things. First, they could use a Cognitive Behavioural Therapy approach to examine the child's feelings and emotions in greater depth and try to work out the triggers for their fears and anxieties. These are then fed into a plan to help the child return to school. This plan, unlike the 'Blagg' approach, would involve a gradual return to school, such as attendance only for certain days or for certain lessons. This approach is called 'gradual desensitisation' but the aim is always to try and achieve full attendance. Sometimes it can be necessary in these cases to arrange a change of school but, on the whole, EPs try and avoid such a move unless there is clearly a feature in the environment of the particular school that is contributing to the refusal. If this feature is not identified there is a risk that the child will simply refuse to attend the new school.

Strategies to help improve behaviour

Motivational interviewing

Motivational interviewing is a series of techniques that EPs can use to motivate reluctant learners who appear disenchanted with school. While most of the young people EPs deal with are open and willing to work with us this is not always the case. Some pupils we meet in school can lack the motivation to change their behaviour and can be reluctant to acknowledge that there are problems in school. English comedian Catherine Tate created a schoolgirl character who, whenever she was criticised, would reply, 'Bothered, am I bothered?' In other words, she did not acknowledge she had a problem and was certainly disinclined to do anything about it. Such attitudes, from a small minority of pupils, can make it hard for teachers and EPs to implement an intervention that is likely to be effective.

There is not sufficient space in this book to give a full account of the technique, but essentially it is a six-stage model to help the young person and their teachers understand how the pupil is thinking, why they are resistant to change and, most importantly, how they might be helped to accept the need for change. The six stages are:

Stage 1 Precontemplation – the pupil sees no problem but others disapprove.

Stage 2 Contemplation – weighing up the pros and cons of change.

Stage 3 Determinism – do I carry on as before or do I change; what's in it for me?

Stage 4 Active change – putting the decision to change into practice.

Stage 5 Maintenance – actively maintaining change.

Stage 6 Relapse – return to old behaviours.

Motivational interviewing contains a great many techniques for helping the student understand exactly where they are on the six-stage model, but equally important is understanding how they can move on to the next stage, or, in the case of Stage 6 Relapse, how they can return to Stage 5.

Motivational interviewing was introduced to educational psychology by Eddie McNamara from Lancashire, who has trained a large number of EPs and others in the techniques. Eddie told us:

The techniques are very useful for those hard-to-reach young people, especially those whose teachers tell us, 'We've tried everything but nothing seems to work'. I have worked with and trained a large number of people from a wide variety of professional backgrounds, including parents, teachers, social workers, family support workers and residential care workers. I have used the training in most of the schools on my patch. What is important is not only the training but also the support that is needed after training when the programme gets going. EPs are ideally placed to support teachers and others in the use of this and other techniques.

In recent years there have been a number of research papers that have shown motivational interviewing to be very effective and it is now incorporated in a number of EP training programmes.

Behavioural contracts

Behavioural contracts are essentially written agreements drawn up between teachers, parents and pupils concerning the behaviour or learning of the pupil. The rationale on which they are based stems from the work of a psychologist called Ron Levy, who found that the people he worked with were more likely to follow a course of treatment if they not only agreed verbally to do so but, more importantly, if the agreement was written down and signed.

Behavioural contracts are especially effective with issues such as school attendance and behaviour. They are usually drawn up at a meeting between all parties in which everyone has a chance to put their point of view. It is important to note that in order for them to work there has got to be a benefit for all parties. Although they can often involve the suspension of a pupil's pocket money or other privileges, what is important is that the pupil can earn these back consequent on certain conditions.

Chris, an EP who uses behavioural contracting often in his schools, told us about a typical case:

> *Brian was a Year 11 pupil who, although reasonably able, found it easier to stay in bed and miss school rather than attend. He had no anxiety issues nor was he being bullied, in fact he was extremely popular and had many friends. His mother worked and had to leave the house early and therefore could not supervise him getting up and leaving for school. We therefore drew up the following contract.*

Behavioural contract

Brian

1   I wish to improve my attendance at school.
2   I agree to attend school every day and have a report signed by Mr Mitchell.

Mrs Jones

1   I agree to withdraw Brian's allowance.
2   I agree to pay Brian 90p for each day attended.
3   I agree to pay a bonus of £1.50 for every full week.
4   I agree to wake Brian at 8:00 am every school day.

Mr Mitchell

1   I agree to ensure Brian has an attendance report card.
2   I agree to sign the report each day.
3   I agree to phone Mrs Jones if Brian is not in school.

Dr Hughes

1   I agree to be available to support any party for the next three weeks.
2   I agree to convene a follow-up meeting in three weeks.

Signed   **Brian** ....

               Mrs Jones ....

               Mr Mitchell ....

               Dr Hughes (EP) ....

Date...........................

Chris continued:

> *It is important to note that Brian's allowance was £5.00 a week and by agreeing to the contract he had an opportunity to earn more (£4:50 + £1:50 bonus). This monetary reward in itself would probably not be a sufficient incentive to change his behaviour but, of course, failure to attend on any one day would be costly (90p + £1:50 loss of bonus). In this case this small intervention proved very successful. I bumped into Mrs Jones some years later to be told that Brian had moved on to a local college and was now heading for University.*

Behaviour contracts have been used mainly in secondary-school settings where pupils are old enough to engage in the negotiation process and they have proved very successful in turning around some very reluctant learners. As Brian told Chris, the EP, at the time:

> *When I was faced with the written contract, I knew the case was up and that I had no alternative but to buckle down. I also appreciated the extra bonus in my allowance, which I had not expected.*

It would appear therefore that the mere act of having an agreement between the school, parents and young person can have an important impact on the young person's behaviour.

Circle time

Circle time is a technique that is used with the whole class of children. Although circle time has been around for some time, it has been developed in this country by an educationalist called Jenny Mosely and has been used widely by EPs in a range of settings from nursery schools to secondary schools.

In circle time, a class of children all sit round in a circle. There are rules. For instance, only one person can talk at a time. In classes of younger children, a child can only speak if they are holding a toy which is passed around the circle. Older children are asked to put their hand up, but all children are listened to and everybody who wishes to, gets a chance to speak. It is a democratic process and allows everyone in the class to have their say. Its use has been encouraged by EPs in a number of areas. One EP, Nora, told us of her experience:

> *I first used circle time when I was a teacher. As an EP, I was work-ing in a very disadvantaged area of the city and was asked to help the school improve their behaviour. Circle time seemed an ideal tech-nique to use. We first asked the children to tell us what they thought of the school and how it could be improved. What they told us was very insightful and helped in the next series of meetings when we discussed school rules, what they thought should be the consequences of poor behaviour, and how good behaviour should be rewarded. In many ways what they told us formed the basis of the school's new behaviour policy. I have encouraged the school to develop the technique to help them address a number of other issues, including bullying and to build up self-esteem.*

Circle time is widely used in schools as part of their regular practice, and EPs in particular have been among those who have developed the technique and encouraged its use in schools across the country.

Circle of friends

Circle of friends has some similarities to circle time in that the whole class or a selected group of children, willing to act as friendly sup-porters, are consulted about an issue, but it is geared to helping and supporting one individual in the class rather than to deal with a larger issue. An experienced EP, Tim, told us about the first time he used the technique:

A school asked me my advice on a 10-year-old boy called Colin. Colin was from a very troubled family indeed. The school was concerned on a number of levels. They were confident about helping with his learning but were worried about his behaviour, especially at playtimes, when he was involved with a number of disputes and fights with other boys.

I observed him at playtime. He spent the whole time on his own and rarely interacted with the other children. He seemed very lonely indeed. Talking to his teachers, this seemed to be typical of his behaviour. They told me he had no real friends in school, although he occasionally played with his younger sister at lunchtimes. I thought that a strictly behaviourist approach to this problem wouldn't work, but I had recently read an article in Educational Psychology in Practice *about circle of friends and I thought this might be an appropriate case to trial the technique.*

Having discussed the approach with his teachers and parents, we set up a circle with Colin's class, but without Colin, who was given a job of helping out in another class. The class teacher and myself talked to the class about behaviour at playtime and then spoke to them about Colin. I asked them for their help. I said that Colin didn't appear to have many friends to play with and it was important that he saw himself as a member of the class. I asked for volunteers who were willing to play with him. Five other pupils, two boys and three girls, offered to be his friends. I later met with them to discuss the sort of things they might do and later the class teacher organised a circle time to discuss 'Getting on with each other at play-time'. All seemed to go well. I followed up the case two weeks later to find it had been a great success. Colin hadn't been in any trouble since he had friends to play with, he seemed a lot happier and had recently been awarded 'Pupil of the Week' for his improved behaviour.

I think the method has lots of advantages. In this case it not only reduced the unwanted behaviour, but helped Colin build up appropriate behaviour, helped him develop new social skills and enhanced his self-esteem. It also had a benefit for other children in the class, especially the five other children who volunteered to be his play-mates.

Restorative justice

Restorative justice is a practice that has been used in schools to help deal with some aspects of behaviour. There are a number of training courses that EPs and others can attend to learn how to use it in schools. It is based on four principals:

1 Respect for everyone by listening to others' opinions.
2 Responsibility for our own behaviour.
3 Repair: developing the skills to repair damage and ensure the behaviour is not repeated.
4 Reintegration: working through a structured, supportive process that aims to solve problems.

Sadiq, an EP working in the Midlands, told us of his experience of using the method:

> *The head of year in a school I was working with told me of a reoccurring problem she was having with two groups of girls who were always falling out with each other and often disrupting lessons with their arguments. It appeared that two girls in particular were at the centre of these disruptions. I suggested that we use the restorative justice approach. We therefore set up a meeting between ourselves and the two girls. It was explained that it was important for all of us to listen respectfully to the thoughts and feelings of each other in an attempt to resolve the issues. Once this was done the two girls appeared to gain some insight into each other's feelings. We then moved on to talk about what needed to be done to prevent the difficulties from arising again and what we might do if relationships broke down again. The meeting went well. The approach is very much a 'no-blame' one and one that is 'solution focused'. We have used the approach several times in the school, with a wide range of problems including a dispute between parents and a teacher. In all cases we have had a positive outcome.*

Working on What Works (WoWW)

Educational psychologists also have a long-standing interest in working with teachers to improve the behaviour and learning of whole classes. 'Working on What Works' (WoWW) is a solution-focused approach that uses many of the philosophical approaches of positive psychology. This approach was first developed in the USA but is now widely used in the UK, especially in Scotland where it was developed by two EPs. The approach is in three phases, as illustrated in the following example.

Phase 1. The class was observed by two EPs. They then met with the teachers of the class. Rather than concentrate on what was not going well, the EPs discussed with the teachers the positive aspects of what they had observed and discussed the ways in which they thought that they might be able to encourage more of this good behaviour. They also met with the children themselves and told them what they thought went well and asked the children for ideas to encourage their good behaviour.

Phase 2. The two EPs then met again with the class and teachers and discussed with them the goals that they agreed to set together to improve their behaviour and learning. The teachers then tried out these successful strategies with the support of the EPs.

Phase 3. Two weeks later, the EPs returned to observe the class again and were able to discuss their improvements with both the teachers and the children. At each step, the teachers and the children were given feedback on how they were doing.

The process can then be repeated through Phases 2 and 3 to iron out any further problems or difficulties. As one of the EPs in this example said,

Because the approach is based on positive-based principles, no criticism is made of the teachers' current practice. Teachers are therefore more than willing to ask for help when classes are proving difficult. We like working in pairs for this type of work and it is proving cost effective in helping reduce disruption and allowing teachers to spend more time teaching.

Strategies for working with 'Looked After' children

Working with carers of 'Looked After' children

'Looked After' children are some of the most vulnerable children in society. Despite a great deal of support and financial expenditure, their personal and social well-being outcomes have remained stubbornly poor. A group of EPs, led by EP Sean Cameron, was asked to develop strategies to help this group. He developed an 'emotional warmth' approach to professional child care to empower and help residential carers and foster and adoptive parents understand and meet the often complex needs of these children. The approach is based on sound psychological principles and research. It includes work on children's feelings of rejection, their response to trauma, the importance of close relationships, and helping parents and carers enhance their parenting skills such as dealing with dysfunctional behaviour, dealing with challenging life events, helping the children acquire social confidence and to make and keep friends. His approach also looks at the type of support such parents need, especially from professionals such as EPs. In fact, regular access to support from EPs is viewed by parents and carers as one of the most important features of the approach.

Sean has called the model 'Pillars of Parenting'. Sean has evaluated the approach in some detail. The responses he had from both parents, carers and the children themselves has been extremely positive. The children appeared more settled in their homes, behavioural issues were dealt with more effectively, the children seemed to be doing better in school and were happier. The success of the project has led to it being replicated across the country.

Strategies to support teachers

Coaching

Coaching is a relatively new technique adopted by EPs in their work. In this type of approach the EP works to support and enhance performance. It uses methods adopted from a number of sources, including positive psychology, where the psychologist attempts to develop performance by concentrating on what is working well rather than emphasising what is going wrong. A good example of this type of approach has been reported by an EP called Mark Adams. Mark was contacted by a head teacher to help and support a recently appointed member of the senior management team. It emerged that the teacher was relatively new in the role and was experiencing difficulties in developing an effective style of management. Mark meet with the teacher and discussed the concern. Together they were able to identify that it was the teacher's confidence that was the key issue. Further discussion revealed that the teacher did feel confident in some relationships but less so in others. In a coaching session Mark was able to help her identify those variables that she thought were helpful in some relationships, and together they explored techniques that she might be able to apply in those relationships that were not going well. This is what is called a solution-focused strategy. In a subsequent session, the teacher reported that she had been able to apply the techniques extremely well and that she felt much more confident in her role.

Developing specialisms

Often an opportunity to specialise arises from particular initiatives planned by the government or by the local authority. A good example of this occurred several years ago when the government of the day was concerned about the standard of behaviour in schools. They made funding available to local authorities to support behavioural initiatives in their region. One of the authors of this book (Jeremy Swinson), who had already written a number of papers on behaviour, made sure he was part of a team set up in Liverpool. It proved challenging and demanding. He was seconded for two years to work with a behavioural team that was set up to support school staff to develop behaviour policies and good practice. He worked with a team of teachers and an educational advisor to develop training packages for teachers, advice for schools, and to act as the authority on techniques and strategies to improve learning and behaviour:

> We found ourselves working with some schools that were, to put it frankly, in need of considerable support, and in some cases where the behaviour of the pupils was far from perfect. This, of course, was having an impact on their teaching and their academic results.

The work proved both demanding and rewarding and led to some innovative approaches that were successful. At the same time, the other author of this book (Phil Stringer), in a different region, was part of a

A career in educational psychology

successful bid to train teachers in how to set up and run their own support groups, specifically aimed at staff concerns about pupil behaviour. Another good example of this type of work occurs in Hampshire. As part of an initiative to help build up children's emotional health and well-being, educational psychologists developed the role of the Emotional Literacy Support Assistant (ELSA). These are classroom assistants who undertake six days of training delivered by EPs. The ELSA can then work in school to provide individualised interventions to support pupils experiencing a range of social and emotional needs. Educational psychologists provide additional training to further develop ELSA skills and they also provide regular group supervision for ELSAs, which assures the quality of an ELSA's work. This programme, which has been well evaluated, gained some impetus from the then government's introduction of SEAL (Social and Emotional Aspects of Learning), which was a curriculum resource designed to develop the social, emotional and behavioural skills of pupils. This was part of a wide-scale professional development programme for teachers running from 1997 to 2011, known as the National Strategies. The National Strategies promoted three waves of intervention: whole-school initiatives characterised by quality-first teaching, small-group support and individual interventions. Although the SEAL project finished along with the other National Strategies, the ELSA programme has continued to thrive in Hampshire and has been introduced in many other local authorities. As it happens, a number of ELSAs have gone on to train as EPs.

Most services encourage EPs to develop specialist skills so that their service can meet the needs of specific groups of children and their families. These types of specialisms include:

Early Years Development. These teams would be allocated time to assess the needs of pre-school children between the age of 2 years and 5 years. Working with very young children requires a great deal of patience and sensitivity as well as specialised knowledge about the various development conditions that can impact on a child's life.

Sensory Handicap Services need an EP who has extensive knowledge of the way that hearing and visual difficulties can influence

106

learning and behaviour. Such EPs invariably work in a team with specialist teachers who can advise both parents and teachers on the best way to meet the child's needs.

Autism. Many local authorities have a team that gives advice on the assessment and diagnosis of children who are deemed to be on the autistic spectrum. These assessment teams usually consist of a doctor, a speech and language therapist, a specialist teacher and an EP. Each observe the child, consult with the parents, including taking a long history of the child, before discussing the case in detail and making a diagnosis.

One EP, Indrani, working in the North of England, told us:

I had always been fascinated by autism since I was a teacher and therefore was excited to be invited to join our 'Autism Assessment Team'. As part of my training I had to attend a course at the Centre for Social and Communication Disorders, which was run at the time by Lorna Wing, one of the pioneers of work on the disorder in the country. We learnt how to use an assessment tool called the Diagnostic Interview for Social and Communication Disorders, or DISCO for short. We use the technique on all our cases. With each new case, we learn a bit more about the wide range of children that can be effected by the condition. It is fascinating; each child we meet is unique but the effect that the condition can have on the children's learning and behaviour can be massive.

Working in special schools

Most local authorities maintain a number of special schools. These are schools to serve the needs of a specific group of children such as those with physical difficulties, visual or hearing problems, those pupils with significant learning difficulties and those with behavioural or emotional difficulties. However, there is a growing trend for special schools to be run by independent providers. In this respect, since they are not directly funded by a local authority, they are also referred to as non-maintained schools. The largest of such providers are the Priory Group of Schools, the Cambria Schools and the Witherslack Group. These groups not only run schools but also specialist children's homes. They tend to concentrate on schools for children with social, emotional and mental health needs, and also children on the autistic spectrum. These large groups tend to employ a number of EPs, which allows them to provide a level of professional support and development for their EPs including regular supervision by another EP.

The work in these schools can be challenging but it can allow individual EPs to develop a particular interest in children and young people with a specific set of needs. Also, because there is an opportunity to work with the children on a weekly or even daily basis, it allows the EP to develop intervention programmes with these young people that may not always be possible within the context of local authority work. There are also many other stand-alone non-maintained schools that are approved by the Department for Education as a special school and that employ an EP, usually on a sessional basis.

Working for national charities

A number of national charities also employ EPs. The National Autistic Society employs a number in advisory roles and also in the special schools they run. Barnardo's is involved in many areas across the country and employs EPs in many of their services, schools and units. For instance, the unit they run in Liverpool is responsible for a number of initiatives, including work with young people who have a brother or sister with significant special needs, work with families over bereavement issues, fostering and adoption, support for families who have been victims of domestic violence, and help for children who have been subject to sexual exploitation.

7 Other career paths and research

Educational psychologists are some of the most highly qualified and trained officers in any local authority. After all, there are not many professions that require a doctorate as an entry qualification. As such, an EP has a range of skills and abilities that are in many ways unique in education. Such skills are in demand across the range of education services. Educational psychologists have a range of experience of working within mainstream education, further education colleges, special schools and units, and with pre-school children, parents and other professionals that is unparalleled by any other group of workers in this sector. As such, there are many career pathways that are open to them.

A good example of the type of varied career that can open up for a trained EP is that of Marc Chevreau. Marc was originally an English teacher, who taught in Essex, Gloucestershire and even Jersey. He trained to be an EP on the Exeter course before working in Staffordshire, Lancashire and then becoming a senior specialist EP in Blackpool. He is part of a team leading a strand of a £10 million programme to help encourage resilience and well-being in young people. He was seconded from his work in Blackpool to pilot and develop the programme, which aims to help 10 to 16 year olds. Marc's job includes developing materials to be used in a whole-school approach and also includes work with looked-after and vulnerable children. He said that the work is really exciting, especially the opportunity to develop and refine materials, evaluate their effectiveness and to be allowed to work at a whole-school level.

A number of EPs have seen the potential of moving their careers to embrace advisory roles within local authorities. Educational psychologists have experience of working in a wide variety of schools and across the age range from birth to 25 years. Educational psychologists have experience of advising preschool settings and schools on how to meet the needs of pupils with both learning and social and behavioural needs. This type of experience is in many ways unique. As a result, a number of EPs have been appointed to advisory posts in local authorities. The number of such advisors has decreased in recent years as local authority budgets have declined but they are still active in some authorities, either as direct employees or as consultants. Another possible career pathway which a small number of EPs have taken is that of ensuring the quality of education in school by become an HMI, that is, a member of 'Her Majesty's Inspectorate of Schools'. These inspectors are employed directly by central government and have an influential role in developing government strategies and policies.

A number of EPs have chosen to train to be members of OFSTED inspection teams. These are the teams whose job it is to evaluate the effectiveness of schools. To become an OFSTED inspector you need to have had considerable experience of working in schools, which of course is the case for EPs, and a particular area of expertise, which, in the case of EPs, includes the full range of special educational needs and social, emotional and mental health needs of children and young people of all ages. Potential inspectors then undergo extensive training and a rigorous evaluation before they become registered and are allowed to practice as an inspector.

A small number of EPs also find themselves working for government in influential advisory roles. After gaining a psychology degree at University College London, Jean Gross taught both in Thamesmead, in South East London, and in Iran at the American School. She trained as an EP at the now discontinued course at the Child Guidance Training Centre in London. She began her career as an EP with a particular interest in problems relating to children's well-being and learning. She then became Head of Children's Services in a large urban authority where she was responsible for special educational needs, and for behaviour and attendance policy. She pioneered working closely with Health Services on joint commissioning of services for autism, speech and language and children's mental health needs. Since then she was appointed by the government as senior director of their National Primary Strategy, including the introduction of the initiative Social and Emotional Aspects of Learning (SEAL), and then as the government's 'Communication

Champion' aimed at improving services for children's speech, language and communication needs. She continues to work on a number of projects on behalf of the government and other national organisations, has written a number of books, and, in 2012, was awarded a CBE for services to education.

André Imich gained a first degree in psychology and education at what is now Oxford Brookes University. He then taught in Swansea for two years, before training to become an EP at Swansea University. This course is now based at Cardiff. His first post was in Newham. He eventually became Principal Educational Psychologist (PEP) in Essex, at one of the largest educational psychology and special needs services in the country. More recently he was appointed as a senior director/advisor to the Department for Education (DfE) for their National Strategies and latterly as SEN/Disabilities Advisor. Both Jean and André have senior posts that can help form government policy.

Inevitably EPs, especially at a senior level, develop expertise and experience in administrative roles within a local authority, often leading special educational needs teams or sections. This gives them an opportunity to have a major influence on education policy and practice. A small number have become directors of Children's Services. One example of this is Sonia Sharpe who, after experience as a teacher, trained as an EP at Sheffield University. After working as an EP she returned to the university to carry out extensive research on bullying in schools. She was then appointed as an assistant director of education in Birmingham, in charge of inclusion policy, before becoming Deputy Director of Education Leeds. Following the transformation of local authority services for children and young people, she then became director of Children's Services in Rotherham and then Sheffield, before being head-hunted for a post in Australia as Deputy Secretary for Early Childhood and School Education in the Department of Education and Training in the State of Victoria. She now works as a consultant with an international consultancy called the Nous Group, who describe themselves as giving advice on pubic strategy, organisation capability and leadership development.

Another former EP, Peter Leadbetter, is now a business consultant. Peter was originally a primary school teacher in north Liverpool. After training at Birmingham and working as an EP, he became interested in helping schools respond to the demands of the changing curriculum and the management of pupils. He became interested in organisational change. After further training he became a consultant with Ernst and Young, an international financial consultancy, and is now working independently. As Peter says:

> *I operate largely as a coach to senior clients, and as a leader of change delivering major transformational programmes, and as a facilitator designing and delivering workshops, events and accelerated sessions.*

He said that the skills he learned as an EP working in schools and coaching teachers proved invaluable in his new career.

Working in a university

There are a number of psychologists working in universities who began their careers as EPs. Perhaps not surprisingly, the majority of these are employed by universities to train EPs. All the training programmes require that the majority of lecturers on their courses are experienced EPs who have had extensive experience of working in the field.

There are a number of others who have been appointed to university posts after training and working as EPs. Jean Gross, who we mentioned previously, had a post at the Institute of Education in London. Professor Geoff Lindsey is currently head of the Centre for Educational Development, Appraisal and Research (CEDAR) at Warwick University. Geoff began his career as an EP in Sheffield, where he became Principal EP. His research interests include children's learning, especially language and communication skills, and inclusion and ethics in professional practice. He is also a specialist advisor to the House of Commons Education Select Committee and thus also helps translate research findings into policy.

Professor Julian (Joe) Elliot, now at Durham University, began his career as an EP in the North East, before becoming a lecturer in education at Sunderland University. Joe has gained some notoriety over his views on dyslexia. He has suggested that rather than view dyslexia as a discrete condition, it is more sensible to help children with reading and spelling difficulties on an individual basis. As he points out, there is no unique programme for helping children labelled as 'dyslexic' other than the type of approaches that work for all children. If you are interested in his approach, you can see him talk about it on a clip on YouTube.

There are a number of prominent EPs who have researched and published extensively as part of their role, either as a previous or present programme director, as well as a member of a course tutor team. These include such people as Professor Andy Miller of Nottingham University and Norah Fredrickson from UCL, who have added enormously to our knowledge and understanding of educational psychology theory and practice.

Working outside the UK

A professional qualification in educational psychology from a British university is recognised across much of the world, and certainly in the rest of the European Union (EU) as part of a negotiated mutual recognition process. However, the number of British-trained EPs working in Europe is small and we are also aware of a limited number of European EPs working in the UK. Over the past 20 years or so there has been a great increase in the number of British families choosing to live abroad, especially in Spain. As a result, there are a sizeable number of schools in Spain who teach in English, follow our National Curriculum and that have need of an EP. Of course, with Britain leaving the European Union, working in other European countries may become much more complicated.

There are of course other communities across the world that see the advantage of teaching children in English. These counties include former British colonies such as Hong Kong and Singapore that regularly advertise jobs for EPs. Jobs also occasionally come up in both Australia and New Zealand. Recently the *Psychologist* magazine, which is distributed to all members of the British Psychological Society (BPS), included adverts for posts in Qatar and Oman.

Very few British EPs have found work in the USA and Canada because of the way in which psychologists are licensed there. This can be a complex procedure in which your qualifications have to be ratified by the American Psychological Association and then, in order to practice, you have to be registered in the state in which you intend to work. The procedure can take several months to complete. A number of

British-trained EPs have university-based posts in America, but one EP we know, Alan Sigston, spent a number of years working in New Jersey for a company called Edison Learning. They are educational consultants who work in publicly funded schools to help improve performance. Alan trained and worked at the University of East London on their EP training course. After his American experience, he helped set up an Edison Education branch in the UK, where he is now Director of Education.

EPs and research

As we discussed in the previous chapter, all EPs have a responsibility for their own professional development. That can involve reading journals and books, attendance at various courses to keep abreast of the latest research, but it also includes many EPs who carry out their own research. As part of their training, all EPs develop the necessary skills and experience to carry out research. Since doctoral training started, many more EPs publish articles based on projects carried out during their training programme. Research by EPs covers a wide field indeed, much of it is published in journals such as *Educational Psychology in Practice* or *Education and Child Psychology*, and also in a number of international journals. There are a number of EPs who have mainly worked in local authority practice and established a reputation for research and evaluation.

Dr Eddie McNamara spent most of his working life as an EP for Lancashire local authority and, along with most EPs, describes himself as a 'science practitioner'. Eddie is widely published and his early research, dating from the 1970s, was into the application of what was then called behavioural modification in the classroom. Together with other colleagues from North-West England, such as Colin Critchley and Alex Harrop, he pioneered reward techniques to help improve pupil behaviour and learning. In the 1980s Eddie developed this work to include ideas such as behavioural contracting, which was the subject of his doctoral thesis (see Chapter 6).

Another approach used feedback to improve classroom behavior. Teachers were coached to simply increase their positive feedback to their pupils, especially positive remarks about the pupils' behaviour.

This work, by one of the authors of this book, Jeremy Swinson, and his colleague Alex Harrop, showed remarkable improvements in both behaviour and learning in a wide range of schools and with pupils of all ages. This interest in the role that teacher feedback plays in pupil conduct led an EP from the Midlands, Brian Apter, to conduct a national survey of teacher feedback by asking EPs from all over the UK to observe classes in their schools and to report back their findings via an internet forum for EPs called EPNET. The results showed a remarkable consistency across schools from all parts of the UK. Encouraging teachers to take a more positive approach towards their pupils has also been part of a range of initiatives reported by a number of EPs who have worked with whole schools to improve their performance. A good example is the work of Ben Hayes, who works both for Kent's educational psychology service and on the initial training programme tutor team at University College London.

Dr Roger Norgate, until his retirement, had a distinguished career as an educational psychologist in Hampshire. He was able to combine a range of interests, especially in children and young people with highly complex needs, with an increasing role carrying out research. As referred to earlier in this chapter, he eventually led the only unit in an educational psychology service in the UK dedicated to research and evaluation, employing three research psychologists. The unit produced a wide range and scope of work, much of it published in professional journals. This included research on: progression guidance (a government initiative aimed at producing data on how well children in special schools make progress); academic motivation and motivating reluctant learners; head teacher perspectives on why pupils are permanently excluded from special schools for children with severe learning needs; the implementation of a nurturing programme; and a fresh look at the scores obtained by pupils on a published measure of academic self-perception.

Educational psychologists have proved very good at analysing the effectiveness of various interventions, especially where approaches to reading are concerned. When the government asked Professor Greg Brooks of Sheffield University to evaluate the effectiveness of what works for slow readers, almost all of the trials worthy of inclusion in his survey were those conducted by EPs. This is because an important part of EP training is in research methodology, statistics and experimental method.

Educational psychologists have also been involved in more specialist research. Recently an EP, Richard Melling, has been conducting research into the behavioural and learning characteristics associated with autism. He has found that young people who have a higher than normal number of autistic type behaviours also tend to have very uneven cognitive profiles as measured on the British Ability Scales (see Chapter 4), which may account for a proportion of their learning and behavioural difficulties and explains why such children tend to be the ones that are referred to EPs.

We have only been able to highlight a small sample of EPs' contribution to research. Because of their training they have been able to evaluate and research the effectiveness of a wide variety of initiatives and approaches. These have included almost every aspect of education from precision teaching, the effectiveness of phonic teaching, critical incident responses, and circle time, to school refusal, teacher resilience, teacher peer support, and restorative justice. There seems almost no area of education that has not been appraised and evaluated by EPs.

Concluding remarks

In the course of writing this book we have talked to many EPs. We asked many of them what they valued most about being an EP. While their answers invariably differed, there was one common theme; making a difference in children's lives. As one very experienced colleague told us:

> *The one thing I value most about doing this job is the positive influence I can have on children's lives. Whether it is helping them become a fluent reader or advising a teacher on a behavioural strategy that helps improve their behaviour, I experience a great sense of achievement. It is sad that we don't always follow up our cases in the long-term, but only the other day I was stopped in the street by a young man who said, 'I expect you don't remember me', and went on to tell me how I had helped him turn his behaviour around in secondary school and that now he was married and had a good job in computers. That gave me a great buzz for days.*

If you have reached the end of this book then we would assume that you have more than a passing interest in knowing more about what EPs do and how they are trained, and you are probably at the point of seriously considering a career as an EP. If this is the case then we hope this slim volume has been of help.

As authors of this book, we have both had long and varied careers as EPs, with ample opportunity and support to follow our respective interests. We continue to think that, because of the variety of activities that EPs undertake and the systems and institutions with which we work, it remains the most attractive and satisfying of all the professions that a psychologist can follow. We have both found working with children and young people, their families and staff in early years settings, schools and colleges extremely stimulating, rewarding and enjoyable. We both think that, often in a small way, we have been able to improve the lives of some of those children with whom we have worked, either directly or indirectly. We hope that should you be successful in applying for a course and in eventually taking up work as an EP you will have as much enjoyment and fulfilment as we have had.

Index